JENNY JOSEPH
SELECTED POEMS

JENNY JOSEPH

Selected Poems

BLOODAXE BOOKS

ISBN: 1 85224 095 4

First published 1992 by
Bloodaxe Books Ltd,
P.O. Box 1SN,
Newcastle upon Tyne NE99 1SN.

Second impression 1995.
Third impression 1999.

Bloodaxe Books Ltd acknowledges
the financial assistance of Northern Arts.

ACKNOWLEDGEMENTS

This book includes poems from the following collections
by Jenny Joseph: *The Unlooked-for Season* (Scorpion Press, 1960),
Rose in the Afternoon (J.M. Dent, 1974), *The Thinking Heart*
(Secker & Warburg, 1978) and *Beyond Descartes* (Secker & Warburg, 1983).
Two poems contemporary with those volumes have been added to
this selection: 'Round', which first appeared in the *New Statesman*,
and 'On the Embankment', which was published in *The Rialto*
and broadcast on *Poetry Now* (BBC Radio 3).
'Man as matter' and 'Altarpiece' are published in their original form.

Cover printing by J. Thomson Colour Printers Ltd, Glasgow.

Printed in Great Britain by
Cromwell Press Ltd, Trowbridge, Wiltshire.

To my mother, departing,
and the ever returning memory
of my father.

Contents

FROM **THE UNLOOKED-FOR SEASON**
(1960)

River rising in India

A man sits fishing on the sultry bank
Of the great river. Nothing stirs except
The earth cracking under the sleepless sun
And fish that lie embedded in the mud.

Looking up once he sees the wall of water –
Hardly believes its power, but if he had known
Could have done nothing. The mile of fields to his village,
Weary to trudge at evening, and all the houses
And many villages and the whole valley
Is drowned in half an hour.

We in a quieter land may sense the rise
Of other rivers, gathering at the source
The wherewithal to ruin us. At heart
We can do nothing beyond watch it come.

In India they cannot mourn their dead
They are too many, and an aeroplane
Viewing the scene notices only sun
Polishing water stretching in its right:
None of the wreckage shows. Why should we then
Lament the imminent surrender of
One among thousand hearts swept beyond hearing?

Eurydice to Orpheus

So we started walking along the passage
Leaving the great hall. Slowly at first because
I was not used to action. It seemed to grow lighter
And with the smell of the sun above on earth
My steps grew surer. O hurry, hurry, thought I,
Lest the dark shadows stir upon their thrones
Relenting that I went so easily.
This time, surely, not as in the dreams
I felt the air – and this time it was true.
Then as even the memory of that place
Was struck out by the sudden joy of a bird
You had to turn. O fool, O fool my love.
The memory of your look I keep with me
Forever beyond sight. The worst is now
I cannot tell you this.

The unlooked-for season

Love, the sun lies warm along the wall.
The wide windows and the smell of the road
Do not say 'Winter'. Ladybirds are crawling
Out on ledges. Midday full on the land
Slows down the progress of the afternoon
Promising evening, like a summer Sunday.

But look where the sun is. Never high in the sky
It crept around the horizon. Ask anyone,
Look at the trees and the calendar – all declare
It should be Winter. Within two hours
The winter night will come up with the fog.

Since you have come and gone in the dreaded season
And left so much in sunlight, I cannot think
Of now as a dead time, only gentle,
With nothing to be feared, if this is Winter.

Danaë

Early the day before she had heard gulls
Crying above the city; the builder's lad
Looked down, an idle sailor, from the deck,
Fifty feet up, of half-made offices.
The voice of the deep sea washed over
Human traffic, bringing a salt wind.

She woke before the dawn, and all across
The vague roof outlines saw the lighted squares –
Gold pieces shining round her in the morning.

Within her father's garden now she walks
Through groves where no bird hops to snap a twig
And reinforce the silence of November.
Slowly without a breeze, from one late tree
The leaves slip on her head, her breast, her hands,
Caught in her hair and laid against her cheek
The last bright coins fateful in the winter.

What use to cast Danaë upon the flood?
The shower of stars falls as the cask swivels
Carrying her over oceans to remove
The love that reached her in an inland garden.
Looking, she sees no sign of the God's love
But knows as doom the springing of her own.

Dead of night

We learn a method by the absence of
The wherewithal to use it. Celibates
Think more of lust than easy animals.
The street-bound man knows the green fields of summer.

And so a larger image fills the eye
Empty of sights accepted, like the walker
Owning a kingdom in a sleeping town.

The swept lit streets abandoned lead
Straight to the city centre, where
Red-yellow-green masks blink and order
Absent traffic down dead-end streets.

Five heavy lorries from the North
Swing from the dark road to the light and back
Into the dark again.

'My mind my kingdom'; but the invader comes
With blazing lights, and into the dark again
Thunders, leaving the absence filling with echo.

The lost continent

A thread of silver marks along the sand
The shallow start of the deep ocean. Dry
Among the dunes a rusty cable points
Two fingers to the white and morning air.
All messages that travel to the land,
Crowded with houses and listening people
Whose life means words, are cut off here, and wander,
Not even sounding, on the empty shore:
The wire no longer murmurs with the noise
That would be words were they interpreted.

Deep within that ocean lies my love.
Once it was linked through every rib of sand
That ran along the bottom to the shore;
And every ripple and every fish that waved
Its tail between the centre and headland
Echoed in green fields. Wrecks became fossils,
The land changed face and we upon the land,
But still the ocean cable reached its home.

But now even near the land sea bed is strange,
Never approached even on calm days
When clearly you could see what lies there.
No word has passed, no tremor felt for years.
The great fish swim unnoticed and the channels
Silt up and shift and make no difference.
The elements are alien and separate.

Sleeping deep like a child within the womb
The curled-up figure of the woman lies
And lost within that passive sea my words.

'Go Back to Square One'

We thought we did so well to leave the house
More or less tidy and with no rent owing.
We left the place better than some, we said:
Minimum fuss without disturbing neighbours,
Not enough damage for a landlord's claim
And most of our own baggage still the same.

Surprising really, how easy in the end
It was to settle down in different towns.
If moving had not muddled up addresses
We would have met to praise ourselves and ask
Why on earth had others made such fuss?
Couldn't they pack up quietly like us?

And then as in the dream when the last step
Brings round the end, only to begin
Without surprise the whole concern again
I found that I was walking past that fence:
Had thought I had packed up and quite cleared out
But only gone a little way about.

I wasn't sure the gas had been turned off
I missed my screwdriver, I'd left some books;
That incompleted letter might be here.
I picked round like a rather stupid thief:
Much worse this time to leave and cross the green
Since I could never tell you I had been.

Then we found we both had business near.
We did not see the house, but now and then
On separate days acknowledged it was there.
We left it well because we never went,
Like blood returning to the famished face
Seemed to forget we'd ever left the place.

The lost sea

You have stood on a quayside in the flat grey morning
Watching the rotting pierhead swim to view
Through mist on the estuary, as if it moved,
As if the sea still rose beneath its boards.
And heard at noon the brittle seaweed crunch
Under the slipping shoes of a tired child
Shortcutting from the village, along the path
Salt has not lined for many a high tide now.

The little railway faltered long ago
Waving antennae over the mud banks
That turned it back in smooth indifference.
With nothing on the other side to reach
It settles now for grass and butterflies.

Ships must have called here often, for on the pier
Shreds of tyres still cling that once stove off
The vulnerable white sides of pleasure boats.
Among the stinking debris in that hut
Beneath the swarm of flies on a dead cat
Remains of nets lie rolled.

Family men in inland garden suburbs
Collected maybe pebbles and precious glass
From what was once a shore.
And knew the names of birds flown South long since,
And cadged sweets from the trippers when they came
And owned the place again when they had gone.

Nobody bombed the place. There was no army
Trampled its heart out. Nor did the nearby town
Account for this desertion.
                    Merely it was:
The land built up here, or the sea receded.

Over the years the fish bypassed the shallows
And those that came the fishermen could not get,
High tide beyond their reach; and the cold moon
Hauled only over mud.

                    The sea forsook.
Nothing to do that would not have been useless.

                        So we did nothing
But watch that shore die as the sea receded.

Persephone returns

I sit on the bank and mourn
Absent friends, the sun
Shining on other walls;
Clouds above different trees.

I sit at noon and watch
The oily light glare up
From flat unlayered water
Separate from all I know;

But most from my good self
That could love the sun and stand
Thought of the endless hours;
That tired, but woke again.

I sit, and in my hand
All the scraps of the years
All projects, all allures
Into the land of the strong –
All suffocate, all drowned.

The old familiar rises
Possessive from the mud
And slips the arm along
The dreaded obvious path –
Once evitable return.

It asks that light should fade,
For rain to hide the dead,
Early dark draw the curtains;
For summer to be gone
Unasking winter come.

Standing I see reflected
Small sun at the Nadir.
With coward's satisfaction
I greet the last chance gone
Of getting to where other actions are.

I move, my shadow thin
Old day in the old way again begun.
Welcomed by the dear familiar, I mourn
Only these present trees now, this local sun.

February floods, 1953

Those who were far inland
Saw, for a moment, the approaching tempest,
A sudden animal raging across the woods,
Bend each tree as a current sways weeds in water.
The roaring beast turned the landscape to a storm track
Till it hit the house, cracked the double windows
And blew the barn door to leave empty hinges.

And this after it had been broken
On the cliffs and high hills that intervened to the shore
This – far inland in a valley soliloquy
Where in stifling summers the stream forgets its escape
And almost ceases to talk of a fabled sea.

It was only when the surprising night had gone,
Like flotsam hurled with an eddy to lodge in a cleft
Among dry rocks news of the broken coast
Flooded inland.

The air where birds unconcerned were drifting again
Was alive with hourly messages from the sea;
Roads linked the land in help to the disaster,
Rivers, swollen miles up, led again to the sea.
Yesterday and tomorrow dissolve at such times.
The delicate structure of sequence is drowned with the land.
These days are in no season, they recall frames
In an uncle's sepia hall – him in a punt
Poling the main street past submerged shop fronts –
But no lives lost there: recall more
The fireman's helmet in a mothballed cupboard,
Recall Southampton burning.

But we inland, watching the buds grow out
Can think but never know what corn land will be like
Where no green shoot will spring for five more years;
And we inland, intent on our sprouting hedges
Can think but never hear what sea pastures are like
With the walls down like pebbles and the tides flowing over the land.

With a fir tree for symbol still to watch in the wind
We have time to collect statistics and erect some comfort
From appeals and tin boxes passed from hand to hand:
But they have only the sea and the tides returning.

Storing a view before the failure of sunlight
We blow on our fingers, and know an East wind coming
Which will snatch the rags of a tramp to reveal a shadow
In our minds, of a king, and there he'll nobly suffer.
Only so, inland or flying over the channel
Hearing the wind or watching the distant water
We glimpse, for a moment, the fullness of the tide.

From 'The building site'

'Walk in the woods at the hour when the fuddled sun
Has still the strength to claim the day for its own.
Rain and winter may soon usurp this morning
But while we can still pretend that the rule is spring
Come for a walk in the woods.
There, through those bushes is what I came to show you;
If you stand on this branch you can see the rotten gutters.
Yes – a shell of a house; the back's in ruin.
Could you think that once there were curtains at those windows,
Fruit-gatherers at those trees, and the sound of voices
Flung and lost in the summer, no mind marking
The echoes of a whispered argument?
No – it was just that there wasn't much else to show you –
A change from your sights in Town. Oh, a friend of a friend
Used to live there. An ordinary family.
Look! Through that door…Somebody carrying flowers.
Did you see her go through that door with flowers in her hand?
A woman with flowers – or a trick of the wind with shadows?
There in my room, withdrawn to preparation.
Perhaps they have weeded the path and mended the gate,
Perhaps now I could…But it's cold and the day has given the sun up
And if we stay here for hours we shall not see
Another trick of the light in the empty windows.'

Wet Sunday

This winter day in spring I climb the stair:
Church music through a door, house dark with rain.
And I wonder if down this wall of quiet ever
Wings on the sunlit air will sweep again.

Now in a room entombed within the house
No dust falls on the clothes across the chair.
Stir nothing in this hollow cavern where
A mermaid stares through centuries of glass

And does not recognise the face she loved
That pleads escape into the mirror, damned
To cross a peopled, air-conditioned desert
And sail on seas that never leave the land.

Here life could creep away, and the sad tenant
Helplessly watch it go; knowing its hour
Was early for desertion, find no word
To raise the heart and work again lost power.

*

Strange that within this room where lamps reflect
A buried space between the attic roofs
And only use for glass is doubling loss,
The pigeons' flattery to summer, moves.

Genus: Homo

Between the stones the human animal
Walks over names, and spits, and growing old
Keeps dim eyes fixed on empty images
And mutters in the streets, and feels the cold.

Beyond the graves and thinking never of death
The youth as beautiful as a sudden flower
Excuse by grace the bold stare and demand
And smile away with insolence all power.

But at street-corners sometimes after rain
A head will lift to watch white horses pass
And see the towers and hear the names of the dead
And notice shadows moving in the glass.

And then again defeated by the sun
Who loves the strong and those born beautiful
And kills rebellion, walks over the stones
Not good, not young, the human animal.

The puppet show

I seemed to see you some Sebastian
Tortured with arrows, but the gathering crowd
Admired your trappings most and saw no blood
Clapping their hands and crying Laugh, fool, laugh.

And like a puppet on a jerky string
You flopped and strutted bowing to applause.
Then when you tried as formerly to bend
And lift with flabby hand the grotesque mask
They pulled you from the wings, they set you down
'To be yourself' again and do your stunt
And shrieked with laughter while you grimaced there
Dependent on their need as on your cord.

And so although you said you hated it
You would not leave and burn in the Green room
The tinsel that supplied your livelihood
Because without it you would feel a cold
Bitterer far than lack of money brought.
Your eye no longer looks for exit doors:
Years of fame and favour call ahead,
Mask and strings have done what no arrow could.

Summer amnesty

Once again we live in a whole landscape:
The grass has grown its height, this year's ivy
Made its full progress round the ruined wall;
The lily leaf has rooted in the water.

And difficult indeed now to remember
The dull face of the man to be shot at dawn
Against a wall behind a foreign city
When we scarcely can recall the smell of the street
In the nearby country town.
                     June in England –
While in a calm sea still magnificent
A liner burns all day in an indigo sky;
                     Fish in the reedy stream
While miles away oil on the water shows
Where rooms of people sank without a sound.

And out there, maybe, on the Menin Road
Each summer foliage is asserting now
To whom the land belongs. I do not know
What once lay under ground I lie upon
But no voice from the cool grass cries out 'murder'.
The eye of the sun views everything, but we,
Seeing the sun, can have one shadow only.

Timetable for a town

I saw a little dog locked in a car
Bursting his eyes with barking;
The sun was scattered on the leaves
And the sumac trees turning.

The window-dresser leered at the legs
Below him, with devotion;
The violet eyes of plaster casts
Stare for an Indian ocean.

The newspaper man who kicks the girls
Chalks up a suicide's hanging;
A window high in the street runs up,
A blackbird starts singing.

Hot air, stale food, fans to the street
The pavements harden;
A brisk smart woman picks her way
Admired, admiring.

The dustbins fill, the flowers fade;
The factory gates are opening
And through the early autumn dusk
Lamps and fires are lighting.

Neon, sulphur and mercury
Throw on the twisted paper
Shadows that no human casts;
The moon sails in the river.

Live lace curtains in the wind
Creep in the sleeper's nightmares;
Oblivious of the moon's eyes
Locked in arms the lovers.

In abandoned lorry cabs
Never wake the dead;
Through the waves of morning mist
Sumac trees burn red.

Recovered from the sea

*'A gold wrist watch which had stopped at 2.35 was found on the body
of an unidentified middle-aged woman recovered from the sea. On the
beach was a lizard-skin handbag containing a handkerchief marked M.'*

The sea crawls evenly, and every inch
It gains towards the bag left on the beach
Brings nearer home the woman in its arms.

Edging her rotting body up the shore
It trickles round the bag and then recedes
To polish pebbles round the promontory.

The watch she wore it has not yet defaced
And when they found the unloved body there
The straight black hands said twenty-five to three.

The clean gold only spoke, only the thing
Of any value now; her voice, no more.
Once she, at least, wanted the watch because

It held her wrist, and now her wrist is nothing.
The dead machine survived her beating heart
Its style still something, but her meaning vanished.

And every living woman could come to this
By slipping, or despair, or anger. Chance
Makes difference in the verdict, not the state.

And anyone beloved could roll up here
Unknown because unrecognisable
For what we think a woman. And no will
Could make us love her, even for what she was.

Tides and the heartless and the change of hours
Polish distant surfaces and leave
Driftwood no longer useful on the shore.

Man in a bar

You see I have been here a long time now
And though the work I came for was years ago finished
It is an easy country to stay on in.
I have got used to the way of certain things here.
They can be absurdly irritating at times
But I get on quite well, really quite well with the people.
And then, they take you for granted. And there's the sun
And the night air in summer. There are the Southern roses.
I am at ease in these frequented ruins
And here at least I have my place as exile.

Oh, I hear quite often from people at home.
Sometimes old friends come out here: I know the place well
And I'm glad to prove of use, I like to see them
But many have married now, and with others I talk
Only of that small time so long ago
When we knew each other; everyone, growing old
Grows old with different ruins, different memories,
Different deaths to recall at the sudden sad hour
When, having talked too quickly, each falls silent.

I have become rather lazy about new people,
And...

No, I suppose nothing stops me returning
Though my brother's family has left and I've nowhere to go
Where I could stay with ease. I could buy a ticket
Between Thursday and Friday, as they say. There's
                                        nothing to keep me
Except what I create. Ah, to go home...
Love is not logical, but has its own
Peculiar philosophy. I know
I shall stay here now.

Whether I regret it, this habit of life that keeps me
Inevitably within its circle, inevitably an exile?
Towards the end of the season, when visitors go
Back to their cooler lands, when sometimes I have

An amusing letter from one reaching home who finds
The garden full of young fruit, goes picnics with friends
I once went with, I in the splendid South
Could break my heart with longing. I do not go near
The station at such times for there are too many
People who go home.
Usually it is in the season before the storms
And had I not, long since, lost all tears
I could weep enough to bring on thunder.

Reported missing

I had a strange dream the other night after I had left you
And it seemed that we were going on a journey.
We had to climb, and a damned difficult climb it was too
In unfamiliar country.

It was rocky, mostly with rivulets, and very bright green patches
And I was always going the long way round
But never got higher; only much further away
From your footsteps' sound.

We were going out of the plains because of your decision
Yet, once above the waterfall, you denied
All thought for the expedition, ignored the ravine
Where the mountain sheep had died.

Suddenly I was in that ravine. Not minding that the ground
Had no real rocks, the clouds neither rain nor snow
I knew that I was lost forever and that
You did not know.

More, that you couldn't care, having gone from the mountain;
                                            had not forgotten
But being elsewhere would have no cause to remember
That terrible but necessary journey
In a bitter November.

I was quite dead in the darkness for a long time and
                              then I was walking down
A bright road that went straight, curved and then went straight
(I can't think why but this was important). I expected
To see you at the gate.

Can habit in dreams work the same as a vision awake?
                                            I knew you would not
Be there when I arrived, I remembered the climb
My vows on the white road, and yet I expected to see you
The same as the last time.

I can't tell you what it was really like on that climb.
But then it seemed as if – I don't know – it's all different now,
As if you never could have reached my danger,
Never wanted to.

Some dreams one knows for such. Even asleep I knew this a dream
Yet when I woke somehow it seemed true.
In sunlight it looks different as I said. I suppose
I shall follow you

On the next climb, get trapped in the same ravine, swear on
                                                    the white road
To endanger nothing again. At any rate
Not my life to one so absent, and again
Look for you at the gate.

Dog body and cat mind

The dog body and cat mind
Lay in the room with the fire dying.
Will went out and locked the door.

Then the dog started howling.
He went to the door and scratched at it.
He went to the window and barked at it.
He prowled round the room sniffing and whining
Put his nose to the wainscot and whimpered in the dust.
The dog body and the cat mind
Locked in a room with the fire dying
And the dog would not lie down and be still.

He hurtled his shoulders against the wall;
He upset the cat's food and stepped in it.
He barked hard at his wild reflection
In the blank window. And banged his head
Until it ached, on the stone floor,
And still could not lie down and be still.

Then worn out with howling
And scratching and banging the dog flopped
To a weary defeated sleep.

And then the cat got up and started walking.

Birthday poem

In the twenty-sixth year of my age
I, two ears, two eyes, two hands only
(But only is enough to take the town)
I, pumping heart that bangs behind the brain,
Two lungs only to breathe the air that pours
Around these ugly buildings, over the babies
Tucked to their mothers' backs, over the feet
Dusty and wrinkled of the skinnyflint children
(Dancing their cherry eyes among the traffic);
That dashes against the concrete blocks to fall
In a shower of sparkles over scaffolding,
Cranes and trucks and sand and rubbish and
Fruit stalls and newspaper sellers, even over
The bad-tempered looking women from Mittel Europe;
I, two feet only, stride into this morning.

And I, in the twenty-sixth year of my age
Lie mouse-dead quiet in a room where harsh
Endless afternoon light shows up the walls
Two moveless eyes glare at. The world stretches
Savanna; desert; forest; dirty towns;
Suburbia; city centre; market place;
Stifling green valleys; Africa, Asia, England.
I, two legs that cannot cross the yard,
Lie heavy without rest upon my bed,
Words lie stacked in shelves throughout the world.
I in the useless twenty-sixth of my age
At five or fifty helpless to escape
Deaf ears, dim eyes, a dragging heart that bangs
Irregular behind the tired brain.

Then I, in the twenty-sixth year of my age
Conquer the world again prone in my bath
Or on the silent stair sing loud hosannahs.
I, rogue and weakling, helpless to be helped
But strong as the changing earth that blows to dust
And then to mud that could have grown green trees,
I, slime and lily, beast of prey and fodder;
I, india-rubber, grubby putty, know-all nothing
Turn, hither-thither, this way-that way, twenty-seven.

Lazarus

That terrible white light he could not shut out
And Lazarus the dead lay on his back
Willing with all his death-in-life gripped mind
That they should roll the thick black rock again
Over the entrance; relinquish him to darkness.

He could not lift his hands to stop his ears
Against the noises turning like screws, and the booming
'Lazarus, come forth,' deep in his brain;
Or move his head to bury his hurt eyes
In the dark comfort of his coffin corner.

The burden of the air falls on his limbs;
And sun and wind, like love upon the face,
Burst in an agony of glory on
The body through which life remorseless runs.

He saw the moth against the blazing day
Heard the sap coursing through the withered fig
And felt the breath in every swallow's bones
Fluttering about the empty cavern where
He now is stranger, as the living to the dead.

He sat at home with those whose faith had made
Him face the world again, and face their need.
But all men marvelling he only knew
The Lord of light insisting that he live.

Round

The body of a child lay in the pool.
'Give me a child' the man said in the meadow.
The lightning flickered in the cloudy night.
These things were ordinary and not uncommon.

The sun had seen the child fall in the pool.
'My child must have a father' said the woman.
The old man saw the thief between the stars;
All this was ordinary and not uncommon.

So short a second takes what years have made.
So many tall men from a moment's dying.
Blue lightning shows what seventy years have missed.
These things are ordinary and not uncommon.

Hot Saturday afternoon and sultry evening
A woman saw her live child lying dead
Another lay dreading her child alive
Every old man's fear came true for one,
And these things ordinary and not uncommon.

FROM **ROSE IN THE AFTERNOON**
(1974)

To keep each other warm

To keep each other warm; eat
To weight the belly, and like cocoons lie
Wrapped away from the street,
Shifting only for comfort
In a long dozing,
Is understandable in dark, in winter,
And it is almost proper that Tom, Dick, Harry
Or even Paris,
No more should give to or want from Joan, Liz, Mary
Or even Helen.

But oh what grace or pardon shall we get
If before winter we hibernate;
If eyes not old but tired stare at the coals
While heaving seas bring down the fish in shoals
About our coasts,
And even the old brown lazy-rolling one
Turns in the pond sluggish with unstirred weeds
To gulp the air
That in its channels myriad movement breeds
But we shut door

Stay close within pretending to be old
Because we cannot bear to face the cold
We know will sweep down through those powerless trees
No country wood but decorative frieze –
They lack protection that can do no harm;
Then soon these walls will stand as square as snow
Whirling before an edgy wind, and so
Neither Tom Dick Harry nor even Paris
Joan Mary Liz nor even Helen could
Be content, and we not even,
Graceless and desperate, keep each other warm.

Women at Streatham Hill

They stand like monuments or trees, not women,
Heavy and loaded on the common's edge
Pausing before the leaves' decline; far off
The railway runs through grass and bushes where
Slim girls and interested lovers seem
Another species, not just generation:
Butterflies flitting in the leaves, not stones.

Nobody asks what they have done all day
For who asks trees or stones what they have done?
They root, they gather moss, they spread, they are.
The busyness is in the birds about them.
It would seem more removal than volition
If once they were not there when men came home.

Ah giggling creamy beauties, can you think
You will withdraw into this private world
Weighted with shopping, spreading hands and feet,
Trunk gnarling, weatherworn? that if you get
All that your being hurls towards, like Daphne
Your sap will rise to nourish other things
Than suppliant arms and hair that glints and beckons?
Your bodies are keyed and spry, yet do you see
*Any*thing clearly through the grass-green haze
Hear anything but the murmur of desires?

Bargains in bags, they separate towards home,
Their talk a breeze that rustles topmost leaves
Tickles the dust in crannies in the rock:
Beetles that grind at roots it touches not.
The women pull their thoughts in, easing like stones
Where they are set, hiding the cavities.
They care as little now to be disturbed
As flighty daughters urgently want peace.

Homo Sapiens

The sun has lost its heat, dahlias
Burn in its stead; brown and tattered leaves
Make way for fruit, at times like a spring displacement.
Earth's secret mists rise and mesmerise.
The lamps burn violet and the tar in the evening
– As one hears said gunpowder was to horses.

But the cat rolls and stretches, not budging, knowing no danger
And women, gorging in gardens on fruit to ripen
The seed within, loll dishevelled awhile,
More like the cat than watching it.

In beech woods husks lie finished on the ground
The stems grow straight for miles, clothing the slopes.
The ripening kernel does not split the tree.
The old cat in the sun has lost its spring
But has no need to climb out on the tiles
Having had thirteen kittens and lost an eye.
It will die when it is kept no longer.
Our downfall is we must be fruit and flower.
Where flowers are for fruit, a second bloom
In a season is rare. We must be husk and tree
Contrive to stand, as if the tree trunk, split
And empty of sap, still drew its life from the earth,
As if the husk put forth the shoot and leaves.
Flabby bag of bones, what hope is there?
We cannot shed the blained and calloused body
Like a burst peapod lightly dropped on the ground.
So wasteful then this garden…

Through the bled body the pale green shoot of the mind,
Breaking the crusted earth – the autumn flower.

Language teaching: naming

Why are we frightened of the word for love?
We feast our eyes on eyes that light the soul.
The word is not more perilous than the dreams
We live on, poisoning the system.
We are not frightened of the acts of love.

I walked along an unfamiliar road
And all around, the birds twittered and danced
Through hedgerows blowing in a flatland wind.
I wished I knew their names and then instead
Of saying 'small, brown, with a spearing beak,
Taking a little run then going back,
Twittering a note that rose to a whistle then sank,
You know, those birds you see in hedgerows
Somewhere along the roads from Hertfordshire'
I could say 'thirp' or whatever bird it was,
And you would know in an instant what they were
How looked, what doing. I'd have caught the birds
In that one word, its name, and all the knowledge
You might have had that I'm not master of
Would straight away be there to help me out.
Naming is power, but now
The birds twitter and dance, change and so escape me.

Why are we frightened of the sound called love?
We talk quite freely about what we need,
We risk enormous punishment when we must.
Is this the word made flesh, rising to grasp us?
You'd think the act made flesh would impinge more
Than a tiny breath made actual through the voice box.
Grammar is power, is witchcraft, is enchantment.
Droplets and air rise from our lungs like a genie
Twisting huge from a bottle to fill a room.
Say 'love' not 'like' (changing tight voiceless sounds
Only a little to get that deep voiced 'v')
The iron gate clangs behind you, and beyond
The bridge in flames, swamps and no road ahead.
We only stay alive on what the word means
So why are we frightened of the name of love?

Some people:

Warning

When I am an old woman I shall wear purple
With a red hat which doesn't go, and doesn't suit me.
And I shall spend my pension on brandy and summer gloves
And satin sandals, and say we've no money for butter.
I shall sit down on the pavement when I'm tired
And gobble up samples in shops and press alarm bells
And run my stick along the public railings
And make up for the sobriety of my youth.
I shall go out in my slippers in the rain
And pick the flowers in other people's gardens
And learn to spit.

You can wear terrible shirts and grow more fat
And eat three pounds of sausages at a go
Or only bread and pickle for a week
And hoard pens and pencils and beermats and things in boxes.

But now we must have clothes that keep us dry
And pay our rent and not swear in the street
And set a good example for the children.
We must have friends to dinner and read the papers.

But maybe I ought to practise a little now?
So people who know me are not too shocked and surprised
When suddenly I am old, and start to wear purple.

An exile in Devon

Deep in English country lanes I walk.
'Herb Robert' she says 'and that's Red Campion.
We have White Campion too, but it's not so common.
Round this bend we suddenly see the sea
And – yes there it is. Almost a Cornish blue.'

I listen to her chatter like a chant
One does not hear the words of. Young and free
She never has known greater danger than
All who watch tides and storms in a peaceful country.
Her two fair children grow where there is room
To learn the names of butterflies and flowers.

Though partly I pray that she may stay like this,
Something in me would like to see her lips
Twisted in sadness, like to see her ugly,
Stumbling to problems that are none of hers.
Her complete niceness makes me very lonely.
If I could smash that fairness she could know me,
If I could make her hate, I could make her live.

Excited with a child's regardless glee
'Oh look at the sails' she cries 'a Spinnaker'.
Here in this haven of peace and Campion,
Herb Robert, wild strawberries, seas of a Cornish blue
I ache for the misery that I fight against.
These fresh free children and green land are none of mine.

Old man going

I do not much mind what happens to me when you have done.
I remember my mother making herself miserable
Saving for a decent funeral.
Death isn't ever decent, and dying's the last thing you know.
I'm sure of that now, watching a stray fly
Crawling over the great far space of thick
Cream gloss paint so high above my head.

I don't mind what you do with the bits when I'm dead.
When you take off this ruddy drip and fold up the tubes
And wheel away the catheter, for the last time Thank God,
And let my stinking body rot in its uraemia
There will not be any of it I want honoured.

Mind you *I* wouldn't want anyone's bits and pieces
But if someone else wants to live like that, they're welcome
To use anything of mine; then again
If you're too old to live you can't pass anything on.

My cousin, of course, she would be shocked to hear me.
She'll see to it all, she's done it for all my brothers.
She'd want to think it made a difference to me.
But it's while I live I want a bit of honour.
My last wishes I won't know about
It's the last but one or two I want respected.

I used to sit on the Green on sunny days.
Which direction would it be I wonder?
Of course even if I knew I could never get there now.
And the women flaunted past, trit-trot, trit-trot.

If only one of them had looked
With something of the look they have when they think they can
        use you,
When they size up the young beef and estimate what they could
        do with this or that one.

That's what I used to mind. All their moments
Riddled with calculations about the next one,
They tugged away their children. *They* would have stopped,
Unconcerned with consequence; but the grown ones think
'If I speak to him now, and he's here again tomorrow…'

I know I'm going on, and you're wondering
If I've got a point to come to, but the nurse'll come soon
And I'm coming to it soon, but what I used to think
About the girls that passed was, they could spare one minute
For a real look and word from all the years
And years and years of minutes they had left.
'What you in such a hurry for?' I wanted to say
'Tripping towards old age?'
                                        I wanted to ask them –
But they'd have taken it amiss. The young are touchy
Not the little 'uns, mind, but the married women.

When I was in that life, I was bitter sometimes
Not having some of it, but now
I'd give you anything to have one hour
One full hour warmed right through my skin by the sun.
Pretty women would go by, and children and dogs,
And I'd bask in the light that shone from their filled round skin
And my heart would warm me, moved by their muscles' tension.
I wouldn't moralise or mind the litter,
I'd feed on it all; life round me would give me breath,
Not the dead air supplied by your pumping engine.

One hour, knowingly.

I went there once, on a very damp day, in the evening;
I don't know why, I just wanted somewhere to go
And I thought of the Green; when I got there it was empty.
The fine rain put at a distance the noise of the town.
Swept and clean it looked; much larger: empty.
Slowly, very slowly, across the space through the grey
I saw a man coming, it seemed from the far corner.
I don't remember he ever came up, though I waited.
The sun would mean nothing to me now. I'd feel uncomfortable
Sitting, disgusting, in all that light. Now
If I think of the Green, I see that grey man coming.

A sequence:
(to C.A.C.)

Catch

Thinking not much of fish, idly at evening
The fisherman casts; heading for sea, swimming,
Casual it takes the bait, sideways, passing.

The fish chokes, pulls; the fisherman engages,
Puts all his play into this sudden catch,
With twice too much for supper can't let go.

Surprised he lands the extra fish and keeps it
Safe in a land-locked pool, where big it grows:
The only tides that move there in its eyes.

The sun has burst the sky

The sun has burst the sky
Because I love you
And the river its banks.

The sea laps the great rocks
Because I love you
And takes no heed of the moon dragging it away
And saying coldly 'Constancy is not for you'.

The blackbird fills the air
Because I love you
With spring and lawns and shadows falling on lawns.

The people walk in the street and laugh
I love you
And far down the river ships sound their hooters
Crazy with joy because I love you.

Even over the flat land

Over the flat land the clouds go
Puffy white, scudding, in the blue spring breeze,
And birds whirl past, raking their shadows over
Bushes and banks and brooks and gravel stretches:
Tillable open land, with few surprises.

The mountain stands, the weather is born from it.
The purity and strength of the dark tarns
Renew the streams that fructify the plains
But secret, at a distance; the hidden plot
Mysterious like a garden walled, blooms flowers
Perhaps once five years, unaccountably.
The unnamed birdsong glories from the rock.

The mountain stood and summoned, with its shadow
Creeping back valleys, pulling the sunlight in.
'This favoured place,' its buried voices said,
'Is liquor of life to you, and you know it.
You may not really look at me for years
But I stand here, I am, and in your being
My basalt glitters and my brackens root.
And you leave for the plains at your own peril.'

But even over the flat lands the clouds go
And birds, though tame, sing by the chattering water.
Sun and showers stipple the varied land
And I leave for the plains at my own peril,
Creep back into the light of common day
And to your arms, my so undemon lover.

Bride to groom

For this ring upon my finger
You take the finger.
With the finger you have the hand

And all the winters it was cold as a child;
With the hand you take the arm
And all it has encircled and supported
That now encircles you.
With the arm the shoulder, and the ache in it;
The neck, stiff, and of a stiff-necked people,
And the soft white throat and the hands that have caressed it.

On the neck this head and its thick hair
And under this thick hair the troublous thoughts
The mind that will not let be, nor let you be,
Woven and packed full of twenty-eight years
Which have this day for zenith as one summary.
And with your hand beneath my breast you take
The pumping heart that will not let me be,
And bangs to the sound of traffic, and the ships,
To deaths, arisings, blindness and betrayals
And will not hood the eyes to tell them morning
Is present in the nightmare, or day the dark,
Yet louder than the trumpets says 'I will'
Over the grey and curdling negatives
Rattling before us in the midday sun.
This day we take each other's past and all things
Hateful and marvellous mounting to this moment,
The point of the pyramid on which you slip
This ring to hold
The broad base, and all our future in it.

The overbold

Trapeze artists we
Our only net our humanity.
Each hold or leap on which depend our lives
We try now for the first time in the air.
Amateur we improvise where
Only perfected expertise survives.

They say that teeth
Timing, balance or breath

Are not the weaknesses that let you down
But that the beam, travelling from eye to eye,
Like star above a shipwreck holds you high:

Looking in your eyes I drown, I drown.

Here lies Treasure: here be Monsters

A child looked in the pool
Where last winter underneath the ice
He'd seen the duck eggs and white pebbles shining.
His eager hand went straight, but, as if blinded
The water clouded and only mud and slime
Grasped his fingers. The pond's grey creature
Swirled in the weed and shivered up his arm.

The mud stirs easily across your face.
The precious stones I surely saw there once
Cloud into useless flint; the guardian monster
Shuts down all access and makes sour the land.

The child would not have nursed his long intent
Had there been nothing there to lure possession.
Without a clay loaded with goods perhaps
No jealous spite would bother to be there
And we could dredge the clear but empty water
Or leave the place, since nothing kept us here.

Non-communicant

A wide river flowed outside our door
Bringing in trees fathoms-high over tarmac.
'Keep the door shut, you can't possibly get over.'
'Where is the river, and what trees?' you said.

All night long the rain and wind upon
The town trapped tight within the occupants.
All night we watched and talked, and then again
'I'll just go out for a short walk' you said.

Seeing no differences you waded through
The shore of rubbish brought against our stairs.
Lack of goodbye was the last I had of you.
'Why, there is no flood at all' your drowned voice said.

Certain weathers

They say love is a great heat.
In these high hot days, then, let us consider the land:
The peony bursts and the sun draws off its colour,
Great unwinking light, morning and evening, lies on either hand;
Iron in the sky sucks moisture from under concrete,
Day after day the noon blares 'Here I stand'.

And love, they say, is like a roaring wind
Reversing the grasses; lain low they reveal
Their white uncommon underside; it lashes
The lake's back to an edge scraping a scar in the bank that will
        never heal.
The animal rages across the country, it is
A wind, like Orpheus, to make the trees kneel.

Then the tired cooling comes, and in the town
Sapless lies wreckage that the winds brought down.

But no one says that love is changeable
The start-stop rain that has us all in doubt;
A sun enough only to bring out flies;
Wind that pushes our hopes scudding from the horizon, now
        promise now wash-out;
Front line forever lost: as finally
Enemy melted – no victory, no rout.

Underground stalks fill as the rain seeps in
The earth withstands the drought and hurricane.

Zenith

The enormous heat has encircled the garden
Raising our boundaries a hedge-height in a week.
Distraction of birds has slacked the string that held
Our actions steady, pace by pace along.
We stand suspended. If we move we fall.
Then we are back and prone upon a cliff –
The mist from the world's cataracts bemusing.
Now we are only a surface for sun, like fruit:
Later, we say, later the purposes.

Perhaps our happiness is like this summer:
Holding, corrupting, laying on the air
A sweet narcotic, making the plums fall
Squelchy, ripe, tasteless when they lie too long.

Men though, more than oranges, can store
The sucking heat of love, and oh what autumns
Active and calm, should our stunned selves provide,
Full of the God, drunk; like Danaë with gold?

No map available

We turned and waved, arms raised above our load,
To those still fretting up the border slope:
'We've got our loot through, see you on the road
If you're as clever', turning to exult
(Aware, a little, that we would remember
This glee, the cluster of guards thwarted, and the valley
        withdrawing
More than stuff smuggled to cheer us through November)
We missed the minute we could still get free in.
We stood and gestured, and the weather struck.
We trudged back to the bottom for another day.

Simply, what had lain ahead was the very worst
We had ever travelled through, or survived, and our joy,
Whirled away by a wind we thought we knew,
Was no help. To have the proper equipment
Was what we needed, or not to go that way.

Nor will this do.
                    As map or record of
That unreliable country we inhabit
It is about as true
                    As the Old Sarum Hitler bombed, to England.
For you
        have come not separate recognised roads with me
But through the marshes seeped your influence.

These sort of stories serve to circumscribe a truth
And lasso an isolatable adventure that has gone,
Tying it into a pattern – mountain, plain, storm. (Enthusiasts
At rest in the evening enjoy inching their way with string
Over the map they have walked) but we
Can't make a foray *into* time (getting trophies, marking routes):
We are clad in it and it moves with us.
You cannot really view the air you breathe,
The egg is nourished from within its sphere.
To organise a symbol for the living
That is you and me wearing our every day,
I would have to wrench rhythm, ignore sense, say
We are the air we breathe, we, following
Our path, are the paths we walk upon.

A version of the phoenix story

A bird flew down from a tall tree
Into my hands, and settling there
Said 'Shelter me

And I will tell you of woods where
You can listen to the bark grow,
To the loom weaving the air,

And when I am strong we will both go,
You on my back, to places that otherwise
You could not know.'

The bird slept and I waited
My hands tied for fear of letting it fall.

When it woke it bristled and became fierce
Pecking and clawing at my wrist and arms
So that I opened my hands after all.

As with a scream it plummeted
'You have betrayed me,' the bird said.
'Yes, but you made me,' I answered.

An animal story

In those days, you know, we had a house with a big garden
Currant bushes, strawberry nets, wild daffodils, nursery beds,
        the lot –
Land on three sides up to the next large garden
And at the bottom fields, then tangled woods.

I remember very clearly one summer evening
Late enough for the heat to have gone out of the sun
Late for us to be up,
This little stranger quite petrified on the lawn
In the middle of a large shaven space and a ring of people
Further from cover than it had ever been.

We were charmed that we could keep the baby rabbit.
We had wanted a rabbit and here one had just landed
And there was no alternative but to let us look after it.
I am sure we took great care.
I am sure we packed it with lettuce leaves
Tried to keep it warm
Anxiously moving its box wherever we went
For fear some cat might get it.

All I remember is our first delight
In finding it dropped on our path
And the sight that, when I think of it these days, appals my
        mind still:
How in the morning all that furry body
Pushed against the sides of the shoe box
Larger in death than he had seemed at first,
The rabbit we had saved.

The grown-ups around us were loving and thoughtful people.
Can it be that they hadn't actually known?
Were they dressing to go out, or how did it happen
They didn't tell us the things we needed to know
To prevent us killing the rabbit that we loved?

*

Fables

1

The gentleman that my black hen lays eggs for
Has diamond links joining impeccable cuffs
And a suit and a voice and a smile of exquisite finish,
But has never been known to express a liking for eggs –
Which is all that my black hen can lay for him.

2

The butterfly is dainty flippant fragile
Like the petal it lands on without moving, while
Man is strong, and marvellous in conquest.

Butterflies cross oceans without fuss
Flitting over arid waters; for us
Even to say 'alas' we need trumpets.

3

This nut withering on the shelf
Enfolds leaves which could contain
Lithe branches, home for singing birds;
Breezes blowing aloft, moist root.

It blackens like an old man's face.
Oh where is the soil and the sweet water
To ease from the crippling shell the shoot?

This small withered nut my brain.

To achieve knowledge, salting away Faust's stock –
Is that better than a certain sort of look
Attained to make another's hackles rise?

Except that the body dies; the body dies.

5 *Jack and the beanstalk*

The boy planted a bean
Plunging his whole hand with it into the earth
Which he was young enough almost to want to eat.
His mother, engrossed with the years, lolled by the shed
Getting out the washing in a practised slovenly way.
The boy dug deep, like his father, and the bean grew,
Planted for his loud-mouthed mother as his father did.
In the water-green leaves' reflection the child and the woman
Laughed in their fecund world,
His shadow contained within her larger darkness.
Incredible that this soft shadow of his mother
Will soon be a lean man gobbling up fat women.

7 *Cutting off one's ears for someone else is wrong*

A man paid 110,000 guineas for Van Gogh's mother.
Not even for the woman who breathed, but a picture of her.
If he'd met her when she was what she was
I don't suppose he'd have given as much to her.

And if he had chanced to meet him would he have felt like supplying
The painter, even with enough sausage for the rest of his natural?
He probably wouldn't have wanted him in his house:
An ordinary functioning man, sleeping and glaring about him.

And although he has to pretend to value her
Saying he'd give his eye teeth or at least his worldly wealth to
        save her,
I daresay he wouldn't really have wanted to give all that money
To have his own mother sitting permanently on his sofa.

A dog would rather have another dog
Than a flat board;

And is just a dog.

8 *Muse*

A great bird is swooping over our yard.
Let her have the chickens while she's mine.
We will do without eggs for many a long day.
Looking into the light to see what bird,
She throws blindness like a rag in my eyes.
On all the air, now black, outline of wings
Is clamped like a sizzling horseshoe, like Mercury
Running into itself wherever I look –
The dark fire that neither heats nor lightens.

9

Stay close, little tortoise, dig in.
Put on the coffee pot fourteen times a day
Day and night intermingled with much slow pottering.
Put your nose out rarely

So that in the spring
There will be someone calm to note the spot
Where my beautiful friend the hare
Died galloping across the frozen hills.
Stay close, little tortoise, stay alive,
Collect your strength, drip, drip, through months, in a phial,
To sing a dirge for our beautiful friend the hare.

10

Fifty-thousand cats cross our garden –
No, of course not so many, but a quantity you can't count.
They are gross and dirty scavengers and disturb the night like babies.

What weather is brewing away in those foreign skies?
For suddenly looking at me through the window
Is this long-haired fluffy grey tiny cat never before
Seen, gazing at me out of a white ruff.
A prize-cat, no doubt, strayed in our mongrel yard.
She gazes sweetly and turns, unsure, away.

11

Think of the minute amount a mouse eats.
The sticky handles of knives will keep them going
Or the bits of grit from a crack in a biscuit.
Really he takes nothing from you.
Insects build colonies from the side of jars
Where the jam has dripped and dried.
Many people think they only take
Things not used up or needed by rightful owners.
What is one smile a week and a kindly thought?
But think what inroads and depradations
A mouse can make. He can gnaw through a wall in a week.
In the end he uses up everything
One ruinous mouthful out of twenty precious books.
He renews his nestful of needs every five weeks.
Think of the eyeless citadels of the ants
Growing as high as trees where no tree grows.
All will be taken after that first nibble.

12

The washing is jerked from shade into the sun
And the rope half-hitched round the cleat in the same swift
        movement.
In the well of the yard stands a woman whose huge haunches
Swivel on solid pillars. Her feet do not move.
Her hands can reach to everything she needs.
A band of sun paints the air by the third floor windows.
She has hoisted the dancing socks from dark to light:
O woman, could you haul me to grace with your strong right arm?

Getting up in winter

The dark is in my throat
Damp in my brain
The ice holds down time's leg
No fire burns.

Limbs uncoil their ache
Tea loosens pain
Gradually the oil drips through
And the earth turns.

Diary

Dec. 3rd Frost   The frost is beautiful
But it corrodes;
It splits up mountains,
It hurts the heart.

Dec. 4th Fog   The blanket fog
Shuts safe within
The wild ark waters
Whirl unseen.

Dec. 5th Fog and Frost   Fog's limpet hand
Holds hard the frost;
Beauty corrodes
Its work unseen.

Dec. 6th Again   The grimes of the world
Suffuse the heart:
Creeping, non-combatant
But visibly brought.

Dec. 7th Finish   Suddenly, distance
And buildings are there,
Sun washes colour
Through vanishing air.

First spring dawn

Apples in the garden of Eden
Must have looked like this:
Red and still hanging when other fruit had fallen.
These in a deserted garden
Rebellion or disease
Seem, now we have imposed the seasons.

But all the birds in Paradise
Could not sound like this
First single soaring voice between two dreams;
Out of the whitening sky,
Winding through sleep, singing:
'Spring now is better than all Eden then.'

Exorcism

No master I but able seaman
Moving for money over the world's waters.

The dark wall high beside the wharf proclaimed
'I am the Lord thy God' in Salvation letters.

I did not go to the clean godly hostel
But I looked, as the posters said, for my own salvation.

It happened that I walked upon the hill
That overhung the quay, a quarter entirely
Packed with little grey houses in long grey rows
A hill of brick and asphalt not of grass.

I found friends in a half-demolished house
Playing cards by a candle stuck in a tin.
I would not say that this became my home
But every time we came into the port
I visited the hill and every time
My ship passed down that coast far out at sea
I looked for the pinprick lights, inconstant winking
Quite different from the beacons of the Sound.
I thought I could tell where those four men were sitting.

One day I called and there were brand new houses
Lighted roads with green edges, a clean woman
Cooking in her own kitchen; a garage; gardens.

As we weighed anchor in a freshening dawn
I pulled my own out of my memories.

Over the years I found for my free hours
A doss in other towns, my homing thoughts
Aimed at another cote. We fished elsewhere.

There was a storm once as towards that channel
We steamed our way. Pitch black the decks awash.
Numb with fatigue and years of passing on

I, man at helm but no skilled mariner
Saw suburb streetlights through the wooded hill.
It saved a shipwreck. Now my clean cool mind
No unhoused vision holds. I wish all well
Within those houses, for there is no pull
To make me cross the road to reach them now
Who once braved tides and captains to do so.

The road from Glastonbury

The holy thorn of Glastonbury sprouted in this dark time
Nearly two thousand years. Spring petals
Float like snow on to the iron cold ground.
They say if you pick a bit when the bush is flowering
It will guard you against all the evils that come.

Bled cold of my fighting strength I turned
Into the Glastonbury road to try my luck.
The action itself warmed me. Cold
And beautiful the winter sun came up.
Thorns that grew thick as my arm hedged
My view of the approaches.
I huddled and went on.

As I went down the hill I thought I saw
Blossom sway high out of reach, above
A little stunted tree knee-deep in grass.

But maybe it was the snow falling, or the strange light
That snow brings with it, deceiving my sight.
And like the world above the snow, how black
How black and empty the road away from faith.
And then I heard the snarling of the evils
Which thought of the marvellous tree had guarded earlier,
Close by the ditches, just out of sight in the dark
They would lollop with ease beside every inch of that track.

Faith and hope gone left only bleary love
Staggering about in the unhealthy wind.

Dawn walkers

Anxious eyes loom down the damp-black streets
Pale staring girls who are walking away hard
From beds where love went wrong or died or turned away,
Treading their misery beneath another day
Stamping to work into another morning.

In all our youths there must have been some time
When the cold dark has stiffened up the wind
But suddenly, like a sail stiffening with wind,
Carried the vessel on, stretching the ropes, glad of it.

But listen to this now: this I saw one morning.
I saw a young man running, for a bus I thought,
Needing to catch it on this murky morning
Dodging the people crowding to work or shopping early.
And all heads stopped and turned to see how he ran
To see would he make it, the beautiful strong young man.
Then I noticed a girl running, after, calling out 'John'.
He must have left his sandwiches I thought.
But she screamed 'John wait'. He heard her and ran faster,
Using his muscled legs and studded boots.
We knew she'd never reach him. 'Listen to me John.
Only once more' she cried. 'For the last time, John, please wait,
        please listen.'
He gained the corner in a spurt and she
Sobbing and hopping with her red hair loose
(Made way for by the respectful audience)
Followed on after, but not to catch him now.
Only that there was nothing left to do.

The street closed in and went on with its day.
A worn old man standing in the heat from the baker's
Said 'Surely to God the bastard could have waited.'

Mirror, mirror

At a certain point every morning
I look in the mirror and see a fair country,
And if the sun strikes the wall
I see a face full of strength and interest
That raises its eyes, and nods 'see you later, see you later'.

And as the morning bustles past
I think mainly of getting to that glass,
To a time when I can let my eyes
Linger along the paths that go curving through that country.
And to this end I go swinging through the morning.

At a certain point in the afternoon
I am led far away from that clear place.
Its busyness is shut up, unmarked; between the glass
And where I am turning, dust and vapour revolve
Obscuring the stairway so there seems no access
To such a remote chamber,
But I imagine the country dissolving,
The towers blurring in the mirror as the light shifts.

At a certain point every evening
I walk up the stairs
Open the door
And stand before the mirror
At last, think I, to revisit
My stored, my cherished, my secret country.

But the sun has gone from behind me
And all there is to be seen
Is a flat place where, one would feel, the air stifles.
It turns out to be a tired sagged face
Mouth surly shut, and whose somewhat ashamed eyes
Glare downwards refusing to utter even 'Alas'.

In a certain small hour
On the occasions when I wake looking for tomorrow,
A gleam flickers through the glass again.

The sketch of a face brushes across the rectangle
Whispering 'today, today' as it passes.

One day
And it could be any next day
The glass will stay blank.

High devil, deep pit

There is a fearsome path in the West Country
An edge of rock joining two promontories
That stick into air, not sea, but as unnourishing
As crags that are washed by salt.

Lovers' Leap, some call it, or the Devil's Tightrope.
They are two lovers preserved in their hour of peril
Forever joined and riven, by impassable need.
One got across, they say, the other fell
Meat for his pursuers, yet they found
Barren rocks only strewn on all that ground;
And she turned stone through mourning.

Even today when a feat of engineering
Has pushed a road along the crevasse bottom
Bringing cars and teas, and a telephone
In case of emergency in a freak June storm
I should not care to be here after dark
Nor linger even in summer daylight, when
The blunt-winged buzzards wheel, knowing their land
As high above me as I above the gully.

There is, among the scratchy crags, a patch
Of close green turf away on the other side.
Did freedom lure the lovers, or the call
Of voices strummed from unearthly rocks by the wind?

Oh dizzy Devil pleasure who shall cross?
Between the gulfs of pleasure on the one hand
And heights of misery to the seaward side
I edge and slither clutching at thin roots.
Would it be better to be trapped below
Turned into stone in a desert whence none can fall?

A meteorology

The wind has been blowing from the Sahara
And dropped summer on us.
The desert that sucks up all green, spitting out only dust,
Has scattered strange buds on our pavements;
Mitigated through mountain passes packed with snow,
Filtered through grey seas,
The stare of the furnace has produced shadowy windflowers,
And little pale stems in our moist woods.

The fierce moment shrivels up thought
Like hay in a brick oven – a puff of ash,
As the melted core a hand that wants it now
Leaving a black shrunk object, like a banana skin in the sand.

The steel is tempered to a salad bowl:
We hold it and offer it, full of green sap;
Fanned through dispersing passages, tunnels
Burrowing into time, the ruinous moment
Might open out to life like these wax beauteous
Magnolias, holding their lush cool cones in the air.

Rose in the afternoon

Not rose of death:
Drawing in to your centre each wave of colour
That your arrested petals give to the air –
Dying inwardly the petals do not fall.

Nor rose of heaven:
Calm at the centre of this city
Monstrous moons, exuberance of stars
Have nothing to do with the light that you collect.
The light of the world has nourished your cut bloom
Drop by drop drawn down into your blood
As drop by drop your root took life from the ground.

Far down the river a cork popples the water
The motion quivers and rocks the air until
Rose in my room you catch and turn the movement
Mote by mote absorbed into your flesh
The vibrant morning tide within your veins.
Equally, hands moving in shuttered clubs
Though no light enters there to give time progress,
Flick flash-ringed fingers as red five black queen
Fall. Seeping through streets this gleam feeds you.

Day by day you calcify, embalming
The vigour you exhale. Fragile you have
Subdued the molten morning in your calyx
The palpitating golden fire that poured
Over the ridges of buildings, right angles, volutes;
And converted percussion of day to this calm strong flowing
Light lapping gentle round the afternoon;
Will equally subdue the night to come –
A ray shooting the dark – into a mere
Closure of a known twilight, not different state.

O rose in the afternoon, your only movement
The imperceptible falling in your blood,
Your vibrant stillness more speaking than all the voices,
If I could give you as answer, my sentence your statement
I would be dumb in peace with the light gone
And only your image waking in the dark.

FROM **THE THINKING HEART**
(1978)

For a new year

Time heals, you said.
It moves, I amended.

But really time fills in:
The great sore ditch running across the field
Bunged full of rubble, of any that comes to hand,
A lumpy scar, dead section down through the land,
In time gets trampled flat, in time glows over
With fresh light grass, and all sorts of little flowers.

Sometimes you see a meadow with a strange bright pathway:
The skin of a weal is delicate and thin.

Here is a place they have been laying pipes
Making, behind the hedge, a muddy desert
That the wind will bleach and set into dry crests.
What are all those little white flowers doing
Twinkling in the clods the men have thrown
Any old how? Have they roots at all?
Or is it the sun flashing on shards of china?

From here they could be flowers or bits of china
Or scraps of litter from some paper chase.
Head to one side and squint, they look like flowers.
Are they the fields', native? will they
Come up again next year when the land has settled?
Or strangely flourish this once, and leave no growth?
Let the wind work for us
Oh let it blow
All the loose dust away, and let
What then can –
Grow.

Tides

There are some coasts
Where the sea comes in spectacularly
Throwing itself up gullies, challenging cliffs,
Filling the harbours with great swirls and flourish,
A theatrical event that people gather for
Curtain up twice daily. You need to know
The hour of its starting, you have to be on guard.

There are other places
Places where you do not really notice
The gradual stretch of the fertile silk of water
No gurgling or dashings here, no froth no pounding
Only at some point the echo may sound different
And looking by chance one sees 'Oh the tide is in.'

Married people going to work

When I am going on journeys
Drawing through the suburbs in a train
Like one clear thread in a garment of heather tweed,
We seem to be cutting into new territory; new faces
Lap against one's vision, people doing
Different things from us, or at different times.

I have left you, and the little stones I see
Beside the track are not shining in your day.
Of the roadside faces and the clothes the people wear
A window flashing, men stopped for an accident,
The encounters and sights that feed you on your way
I cannot be, for hours, participant.

But the world is round.
The track of love I travel brings me back
To a station where we have been
Where you stand and wait, holding out your hand
All the goods of your day on offer
In exchange for all that I have seen.

Anthropomorphism reversed

The vacant lot has long been vacant.
When the mask of frost that here furs over
Disgusting things, anaesthetising rot,
Shall have seeped away in pools, leaving
Perhaps a green of grass in other places
This tumble of bricks, bottle bottoms, cracked tarpaulins, dog bones
Black bones of scaffolding propping one side of this strange garden
Will be as indistinct, as unlustrous
Wearied beyond even stench, one feels, – decomposition too active
      for it –
As now when iron cold pre-empts colour and movement.
Then even moist limp yellow straggles
Of old summer's grass lying on stones like hair
Will have lost any gleam or grip.

But I look at it after
Days in the grey womb of a fog-like house,
Protected, beating slowly only, in sleep.
I look at the utterly frozen countryside
That strangely has these sheds and buildings on it
Not seeming like a town, no movement shows
Except the distant slicing blades of light
That fall, glass icicles, from the wide open sky.

And I think, if a pushing season can change our hearts
And birds and buds effect a loosening
Before the earth is ready to thaw or stir
Could human hearts in love bring on the season
As all our breaths in separate rooms in London
Must warm a segment of the atmosphere
Making a pocket of another climate
Where hyacinth can bloom and limbs uncurl?

ALTAR   PIECE
A meditation on lust, desire and love.

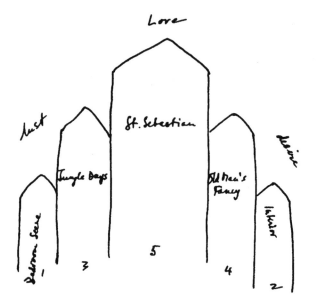

Love

Lust

St. Sebastian

desire

Jungle Days

Old Man's
Fancy

Bedroom Scene

Initiation

1

3

5

4

2

Altarpiece
(a meditation on lust, desire and love)

STUDY: *A lady in her bedroom* (Bonnard)

'Mirror mirror on the wall
Who is the most beautiful?'
If you hear the answer 'You are',
It doesn't come from the mouth in the mirror

That shapes not words but silent kisses
To someone not there.

From hands the answer rises,
As you rise from the bed
Making no noise, no interruption
They move over you in the air
As wax coats cheese,
They stand you up shining there
Before the mirror
Shaping and preserving you as beautiful
Because they feel you so
That you see through what the eye says
To the body the hands have made
And this it is that prays
'I am, I am.'

INTERIOR: *The man turns the sheet for the musician* (Dutch)

Too many beautiful women lie alone in bed.
The mirror gives no answer to these, the air
In boxes where one human breathes, grows withered
And cannot carry an echo through the room
In answer to the question 'Am I fair?'
Fair...

Only the use of beauty will preserve
Your beauty.
The vampire lust sucks bodies limp and lightless
But my desire will silver the mirror where

Your new-lit eyes, not seeing, will declare:
(From any unadorned, uncastled wall)
'Made in my image, while you look at me
The answer to your open mouth must be:
"You are the fairest of them all".'

LANDSCAPE: *Jungle Days* (Dutch)

It is good to attend to the flesh and groom the pelt –
So smile the smile of the cat that has licked the cream –
And grin with the tiger that has swallowed the hunter –
And laugh and glow with these young men at the ready
All smoothed for Saturday night.

For it is complicity with death the enemy
To undermine those reinforcements
Drummed up to reassure the population;
To be a rat that gnaws through the sandbags
Stacked, generation after generation, to harden
Into a wall against the desert's onslaught.
O do not say this is not the defence that's needed
Nor point out the futility of setting sand to sand:
It has been used for years and is acceptable.

Be happy therefore with the lingering postman, pleased to present
The envelope (pools win?) to housewife in doorway.
She leans with her house open – warm street, warm welcome.
Summer is here, shut no doors now, we say;
Pass on the happy cliché and it might turn true.
Never mind who gets the whey
We don't know the hunter
It wouldn't be one of *our* wives young men go after
(For see, we will join them and of our share make certain).

We have kept out the desert for *our* green to flourish
We have trained and suffered –
Not to learn how we can live off rock
If that should prove to be all there is left to live off,
But to grab a valley where and when we can.

So if you have chanced to see a cat with a bird

That flaps its wings with its head stuck down the cat's throat,
If you have seen a mauled and gangrened arm
And smelt its ripped cargo rotting in the lianas

Think of the worm
Think of the bloodstained beasts.
It is their nature to do so, is it not in yours?

And if your talent is to smell the rot
To know where the cat has been, lithe creature, and divine
What happens in lodging houses in the week –
What the young men look like when they cram their mouths,
Don't tell the children the things mirages come from.
They may need one to get them across the desert,
And miss the sweet mouthful that could have kept them going.

But wise and ugly, circumvent the ice
On which the eleven day feastings have been set.
It is good to attend to the flesh but the Thames melted.
Solid as that the mirror in whose blue veins
Shine the smile of the cat, the grin of the tiger
The nice fat woman at her door, promising,
And the glow that their movement strikes from the limbs of the
       workers.

ALLEGORY: *Old man's fancy* (Poussin)

If I could slide my hand over your thighs
Fashioning round the haunches of the land,
Smooth green pelt that rises to my touch
From the white headland chalk bones that I finger,
The young trees opening to my loving breath –

But only rain and sun can make the grass grow
And I am an old man now.

If I could lie on the beds of your running rivers
Stretching my limbs through the valley folds to your farms
Secret in woods far from the wind off the sea –
(The giants in those days had bones that, turned to chalk,
Became these hills)

And let your waters pour down over me
Winter and summer till I calcified
Like a statue on the stones,
Perhaps the juice that fattens out the grasses
Would strengthen me and liquefy my veins
And I would breed a race of beauties
Living by your streams among your woods
Offspring of god and land,
Standing on your bare hills with their long hair gleaming
Blowing about them in the blustery winds,
My bones beneath their feet.

But only life can make the living grow
And I am an old man now.

Sitting in the car with the window down
At the spot my children brought me, to see the view,
I cannot even bend to feel the earth
Covered in its green fur, dry and springy.
My giant appetites towards this land
Are greater than its children need to feel
For they are of it and I love them too –
Soft creatures I have brought out of the grass,
My nymphs, my grandsons who content each other
And do not know the racking of the Sky God
Pressing on his more than human earth.

CENTREPIECE: *St Sebastian* (Italian)

Faith struck Sebastian, got him
Hands twisted behind his back,
His heart thrust out
And other vulnerable parts he could not cover.

Now see Sebastian a prisoner there
The archer's patron by the archers hit
The soft white skin no day had looked upon
All parts exposed before the clothed crowd
Stretched for the tough little darts and the shafts of eyes
Armpits and groin tied open for their arrows.

The arrow of lust has hit him where it hurts
And he has no protection, for he looks
Upward into another element.
Died for the cause, for preaching love to men
Caught by the unconverted, no defence
And all his caring turned against him now.
Love tied his hands. He cannot catch the darts
Hurtling towards him and return them back.

It is not hand alone that shoots the shaft
Into the entrails of the body of love.
It was the word of Brutus, not the sword
Left Caesar undefended.
The word, like the barb on the shaft, feathers the dart
And fixes it in the skin against withdrawal.
They left him dead, relieved to have rooted out
The alien soldier from their body of men.

But love that stood him there thought otherwise.
Strange the seeping word, for lo at night
Sebastian carried to a little place
Where quiet and sure his wounds he struggles from
Helped by good women, fleshly life long done.
Set forth again by kindness on his voyage
Straightway to General Diocletian went
'Your servant, left for dead, reporting, Sir,
Ready for service, for see how little harmed
By arrows of the world my intent was.
You must believe me now, for here I stand.'
'His head it is supplies his lusty flesh
With all this lofty life and resurging.
Batter it then and see if *that* survives;
And pulp his secret on the cobblestones.'

Portrayed again and this time on a boat
Hands tied behind his back, glazed figurehead
Breasting the wave with white flesh, cherry lips
And freshly glossy dark black cherry ringlets.
Figurehead for heroic acts, bright log
That faltering worshippers tie their goodness to.
So let the ship depart on its endless voyage
Cracked and warped as it is with the summer pestilence

That swells tongues in the back streets of the town
That bloats the corpses in the sewers thrown,
Ricocheting disease, flesh stuck to flesh
Clinging to what it takes its fever from.

So out to its plate of water where no land
Can ever creep up round the horizon, where salt
Dries out the festers, shrinks flesh, where the thongs crack
And Sebastian's hands burst free. Above his head
They soar, and like a swallow flashing
His body shoots from the deck. In a perfect dive
His encrusted body of death he draws through the green
Green wave. The mighty ocean takes him.
At last upon his proper element
Embarked, immersed in waters, laved in love
He can make use of all adversity.
Buoyed up with salt and love, O he rides over
Six little waves to roll in each seventh seventh.

'O all you worshippers, locked far inland
O you may keep the images of my flesh
And let help who it may; the rigours of love
I have gone through have freed me to a life
To use my body as I know it best,
Not bodiless adoration, but embodied
In every turn and twist, the dolphin's lair,
Directed by the thinking heart, so now
I run with the tide, and this great tide runs high,
This is true worship, to breathe, to act, to be
Part of this running tide, in love set free.'

The much-garbed painted crowd cling to each other
Pointing and looking at the empty hill for their saint.
Far off between the hills at the end of the picture
The noonday sun sparkles on the little waves.

Love and Justice
(to Barbara Grant-Adamson)

Justice we ask
From grey-clad, clean-lined figures,
Not talking overmuch, standing in line
Or sitting upright, looking with a clear stern gaze;
The known; and we can take it – no tooth and claw –
To give us what we say we want: our rights,
To see to it that each gets his deserts.
You can count quite clearly what there is to pay.
We nod, draw in our breaths, and do without thereafter.

Justice is all we *can* ask:
To feel we can reckon the number of stairs, the length of the passage
That the world is knowable and can be tamed
That we compete for a place in that strange bed
Where every traveller's fitted, and cripples made.

With justice we can claim.
Without it there's no road that isn't mined,
But darks and deeps and stumbling off the track –
We don't expect to be supported *there*.

But when the moon sails clear of encroaching cloud
And seems to show a firm dry road ahead
Oh who would not rather run to love than justice?
Procrustes' guests and Cinderella's sisters
Could after all not walk in the streets or dance.
Justice keeps up a world based not on love.
Without its hardcore we should sink in the bog.
You cannot ask for what is sometimes given
Nor claim, but hope, for more than you deserve
When you visit the hunched inexact domain of love.

Trying to understand violence

The fly is not a nuisance to itself
It is fat and beautiful to its own kind.
Happily it hovers over the meat
Taking off with bounces, buzzing with joy.

In the heat the pavements blotched and stained
Stink with the market offal, and the flies
Cluster round the garbage and our legs.
They will choke us if we do not kill them.
Ugh! they are crowding over the food, inserting eggs
Into the meat and smearing it with danger.

To hurt humans is quite different, they do not
Rot our substance; the bayonetted babies
And other innocents thrown to the cobblestones
Did not threaten the soldiers; but those men
Had been told they did; taught disgust
They swatted them like flies; the eggs would grow
Into a horde to overrun their land.

This sticky gritty wind infects the air
The streets are full of vermin, and ugh! – these flies.

Meeting up

See, it is all one thing, now, this meadow.
The cows strolling about have lain down in focus
It is perfectly right there are more here than there.
The bird is flying into, not over, the centre.
Canals thick-standing in static air, meander
With just direction and pull the grasses together,
The hummocks, the flitting butterflies, the cowpats.
From the right hand of this picture comes a tractor.
Its sound lassoos these objects as the track
It's going along frames the field, and winds
Through the wood off left. You cannot see
But know it goes out again, and comes back round
As arms of love hold in eccentric movements.

And look, we're here now, me, myself and I
And parts and pieces unanimously stand.
Bits pared off on the way, components dispersed
Attributes, intentions, seemlinesses,
Stripped off, stamped underfoot (and the skin grows over)
Caught up mysteriously across the years,
Creeping where no path showed, where I thought
Unmaintained and functionless they'd rotted
Into the waste-tip of the severed past.

I stare at the water-meadows to grasp, to hoard
The whole within the glass before it blurs
And from this centre send my mind's rope in
Increasing circles to include this boat
This mud-flat, now the island, even the slope
Beyond the estuary on the other side –
Not added but included.
The cows, cowpats, hummocks, grasses, birds
Are as they were.
They are no more unified
Than every separate beanflower in the field
That in their difference pulled my mind apart
In earlier years.

They
Are as they are. The stanchions of my thought
Have drawn them in together to reflect
The monolith I need to circle round,
To hold the deep-sea netting of my mind.

Lost hold

I stepped from a bank with sea pink and long tufts
Of separate grasses, the blue day all about me.
Between two steps I saw the earth so clear
Each grain separately winking, heard every leg
Of insect creaking, and every worm that breathed.
And in the cradle of my mind I held –
As I might nestle a perfect stone in my palm –
The open secret of the world at large.

And edged as was the bright sky was my mind
With clear and solving ever-meaning words
The kernel of this great truth greatly to show.

Two steps along the track and the words had gone
The day and grasses faded to a beauteous
Example only of a lovely land.
My pebble out of water has no lustre;
Seems, shown to you, to have no point at all.
The shore is dark now, my mind gone again
But somewhere must the pulse of light be lurking
Pushing at flaws to break through. Is it under the skin
Of the stone, or wrapped in the mesh of the mind?
Is there a good sharp blade to cut it free?

The Goddess of Nature's diatribe to her people

So you thought those gorgeous lips were for you to use?
Made for tasting, made to bring you delight
And equally to those who gaze and kiss?

You think that rose
Unfurling petals stiff with creamy life
Is for the onlookers to rest their eyes on!
That the clambering lily shaking off the mud,
Fun in back streets,
Love out of suffering
Is the apogee of mud, slums, suffering.

Why should I wonder that you are such fools
Since even this foolishness I planted in you?
Your pleasures are planted on you like Nessus' shirt.
Screaming with agony you tear at threads
That nowhere are removable. To move
Back up the worn moist step that you slipped from
Into the liquors of the hypnotic flower,
Would pull your flesh off; body, the self's clothing
Meshes your substance at your every wriggle.

Look at those insects drowning at the heart of my flowers.

Think to avoid me? Going to get the honey
Without the sulphurous smoke and swollen hands?
Think to refine the juice of love from its smell
By breeding out the strains that bind you so?
Whichever came first the egg is not a by-product
Of hen who lives a separate life as hen.

Nothing's for fun – for my convenience only.
Little ants, toiling up a self-made hill
What gratifies that you meet, oh savour it
But do not turn and bask in it as aim.
Pursuit of pleasure leaves you trapped in duty
My slaves.
One little brush against the sticky side
And down you go into the seething centre.

An answer from her goblin

I work in your kitchens
Yes, I am your creature
I see as much of the sky as you want me to
You raise your eyebrow and my left toe twitches
I run up and down clattering at your commanding.

But listen here, old bitch, tho' I know you've got me
I forget, on occasions, I'm bred in your arrangements
And I have valued the bent and awkward and have not ministered
Always to the strong.
I have not at every point slavered
At the lips for pleasure in front of beautiful witches.

Tyrant, in your accounting you have forgotten kindness
The little decencies between spent beings
Tending each ordinary heart
Wrapping the sobbing body in the soft blanket
Of everyday thoughts from those who grieve alongside.
'I too' the broken say 'I understand.
Come and rest and gain a little courage.'
I stoke the fires. I follow the regime.
But I am storing up my fighting fund.

The Goddess goes on regardless

Extraordinary defences against Me!
I'll get you born, I'll make you stretch to the light
I'll let that light corrode you.
All that lovely food you champed and champed
Not able to resist, the tongue salivering,
Dripping to merge with the juices of delight,
Spurting from greed to greed not satisfaction,
Has gnawed you as it fed you, and at the root
Of your devouring appetite the weevil of pain
Is sitting waiting in bone's antechamber
To burrow into the instruments that demanded
More and more pleasure – organs, glands and fibres.
My torture chambers wait for those who turn
And equally for those who fawn on me.

Nothing but hazard can keep you from my rake
And even that mindless wheel is spun by me.
My logic is that fact should follow fact
Only 'it is so' sounds through all my kingdom.

A grinding work for nothing but waste, you say?
And where have you seen peaches and dawns like mine?

Against the personality cult

Kind of you, sunshine, to come out just now
As if for us, materials for pattern making
Suddenly laid to hand.

The thought is that someone in control
Is sensitive and amiable to our needs.
The point of patterns is to be thorough, to recur, to conclude.
This one goes on: sun mist dark dull days, and open eyes
When we are nowhere.

So shine, sun, bless you, but not for us.
Shine only, and I hope I'll be there.

Life and Turgid Times of A. Citizen

PROEM: *Against metaphor – but how then?*

I am not going to talk to you about islands
Or about waving grasses.
I am not going to mention the lakes that the moon fills
(Although there was a moon this morning, a very fine one)
Or talk about doors closing when I mean heart seizure
(Although no doubt you shut the door when you left)
Nor refer in this season to a window opening
Nor of blind choking fog when I mean an adult crying
Crying, crying all night.
Oh no, if I want to say louse, pig or bastard
That people are bullies and like to watch others fall
On these broken pavements, and never lend a hand
Except to keep themselves up, I should say their names.

I will not watch the woodland lake dry up
'These four walls' I will say 'and no one here.'
(That's empty enough. The woman tried as hard
As anyone ever did. She bore no grudge
She didn't lie or nag. But so he left her
One lung and four kids; cotton dresses from the summer.
He needed, he said, someone a little more cheerful.)
Nor hang-glide round the cloud crags of a sunset
'Light falling at such degree' I'll note 'on cumulus.
Soon to be dark.'
(When it is dark the people who have no homes
Become vagrants. When no business is doing
– Shops, libraries, offices, surgeries and bureaux –
They fall into a category of the dark:
Vagrant, not man or woman standing there.)
I will not listen to the wind in the yard what it says
(Tell me again: the voices I hear are lies.)

I'll give you these streets, these lives, these shops, straight.
                                                    Right?
The gobs and smelly flesh; the pleasant touch
Of people pleased to be warmed in bed; the fear

Of others taking what we yet might get; relief
Of the treadmill holding the foot again, secure.
And if someone is kind or beautiful
I will say so, and not talk of sunlight
Slanting down afternoon walls;
And the bustle and beams of lust in passers' eyes
Cherishing the day, quickening to the music
When other people play it, and the race in cars
Along the splashy roads and out and away:
The poise, the gearing, the rise in the blood and hopes,
Flick of a mobile wrist, swell of a breast
Shirt open on a pulse in a neck, warm breathing.

Ah no, we have gone too far
I said I would not talk of roads, of routes
Of night drives over the flanks of the land to the heart
Of a strange countryside in a hidden valley.
This town is on a map and it must stay here
One street much like another, and the hour
Of nine, say, on each day of the week the same.
Here's your piece of paper. Who lives here?

The town on the map has left out the dirt and the people
And the fact that things move, that daylight comes and dies,
That feelings waver in and out these hallways.
They have omitted to mark what the breath makes:
Islands and waving grasses; what the heart looks for
As sun makes shadows on an empty wall.
They do not know the corners which we round
Trudging home, our strength knocked out at the knees
Struck in the bone by circumstance; the ledges
That contain a whisper in the air about them
Matching some susurration in our blood
Which, while we feed it, says:
Piece of earth shoved here and there in the wind
Barged at by bullies, fostered here and there
Little thread weaving in and out of a day –
Citizen of this parish: the island, the hour;
Listen to the voices, watch the wall;
If you can hear my singing you are welcome.

Chrysanth

You see all those words thick on endless shelves
Stacked in their dust, thin poles in a forest stretching
Along straight lines marching to the horizon
Nothing but conifers covering the whole world
Black specks, leaves, words, squiggles on a white-board sky;

And you see that chrysanthemum
Suddenly a pretty blob against a fence
New since I last was here?

It is the chrysanthemum I want.

Chrysanthemum is pretty
It clears the eye
Eases the brain
With wayward movement.

Wind comes, lashes, bedraggles;
Eye and joy dull.
Somewhere in these books, goddammit,
Unfurls, dancing –
Bringing back all still autumn mornings
Bursting from those tight crowding pathless straight stems –
Luscious chrysanthemum.

Moon in the morning

Winter moon
You have sailed into the morning with me
Watched all the time I slept
Waited into the daylight till I could see you.
Prepared to lose your power
Miss your journey
In the face of day
And hung for one moment of clarity
Your open face into the open basin
Where night-being and day thoughts hold together in me –
Skin and silver water.
If now I look for you there is only pale blue and pretty peachy light

Steam and tiny traces of smoke
Clean in the air; and red and black roofs gleaming.
The day full of objects is scrambling our communication.
They have taken you down
The clear basin covered and dark now.

Waking

I am making a cave
I am making a cave out of
Out of the borders of sleep where daylight and birds
Push through the grey.
There is dancing and activity
And a fire that throws shifting shadows
On to the wall of the cave,
The cave that I'm clinging to
With every bit of my body.
I am trying to keep
I am trying to keep these shapes
These shapes I must fix, hold on to
But a great white smoke blows in.
'Cup of tea for you. Cup of tea. It's hot. Don't waste it.'
I am hauled into empty day
Bereft of my dreams, of my story.

'But they could do something about that'
(in praise of the bourgeoisie)

The fragmentation of good gear is sad.
I am sorry to see the gold objects go
But some of them can be replaced, and of some
I have made replicas of steel which serve.
What I regret most
Are places not made pretty, plans
To fix things, and the pieces of wood, lying there
Till rotten. Talk of outings;
Syllabuses not books;
Pots still waiting for roses to ramble out of...
The dreamy primrose path so dreary-sided.

I think of Italians in cramped tenements
Making a hanging garden on rust-stained concrete.
If you look up the cliff from the alley well
Catching a glimpse of geranium, you sense a blue
Of hot sea shore, sniff and sparkle
Of windows opening across bays.
                                        I think
Of people who clear their basements and lay carpets
Make fences and straight paths and box in pipes.
On a tin tray, dented and paint peeling,
The Japanese build a flourishing garden of ease
With little bits of glass.
They made belts out of sweet wrappers in the war.
They collected waste paper and it actually got to the depot.

This house is full of half sets and broken tools.

Tripping down
(SCENE: *Another cold hillside*)

I hold this goblet under the running tap
And it sparkles, being cut glass, and the droplets of water sparkle,
Beautiful as a chalice Morgan le Fay might bear.

But the water should be hot and isn't
I should have seen to the boiler
I should have done the washing
I should have eaten and not drunk.
Damned domestic skills
I would rather have Morgan's starveling ones.
How long can we live on cold water running over the rim
Of a beautiful goblet?
Ah, for a long time, I could, if holding it high
Running freezing over my hand with the boiler out
I was really looking into your beautiful blue cut-glass eyes
Instead of – old post-party trick – conjuring
Down the long tunnel of my own brown pebbles.

A patient old cripple

When I am out of sorts with the things
The world is made of, and box lids
Come off with a jerk sideways, scattering
The little things I can't pick up
Screws and buttons, bits of paper, pencils,
I think how I so loved the world once, as did someone else,
And remember hands that are beautiful – In pictures:
Soft and straight; fingers with tender pink nails;
And hips and legs an advantage, not crisis, in women.
Then I think
To birds my hands would not be hideous
A useful claw (they would see) not white
And strengthless and slabby and straight—so unprehensile.
The hand of my grandchild and mine are the same thing
As a word said differently is the same at root.
I curse the world that blunders into me, and hurts
But know
Its bad fit is the best that we can do.

Inverts

There was a woman
Who moved crablike
Humped in two directions, so bent
You'd think the front of her shoulder would graze the pavement.
She pushed a cart
With four or five mangy scrabbling dogs hued,
Like her, colourless.

I never saw anyone help her at the curb
Nor carry the bag that pulled down her other arm.
Perhaps it balanced her or was fixed on.

On busy pavements there was always space round her.

Later I saw her without the dogs, more bent
As if some engine slowly wound her tighter.
Their removal had not helped her but perhaps Health
Had some consideration in plague-free streets.

I recall, though spring is far away now, some buds
Are very curved and shrivelled, pale at first
And straighten into beautiful crisp flowers.

Oh idle beauties goldened in the sun
Do you not think your harsh and bitter laughs
May not wither and shrink those inner tendons
Fleshed now in comeliness and right proportions?

The little twisted woman trundles on
The young men sigh because they cannot move.

Not able to resist the spring

There is too much stuff here:
Everything crowded, duplicated, and far too many words.
If I could just lay one silver blade across the sand
This would be your message –
One blue vault
One opposing ochre curve
One small man-made artefact drawing them together.

But I live in a crowded place
Myriads of wings and insects try for the sun
And the earth is traced and heaving with soft green spurs
That are uncontemplatable in terms of counting.
With all this buzz and batter and life drifting in clouds around me
Every breath full of mites and husks and voices
How can I only point one finger once?

Chorale

Oh what a syllabub
Hubbub
Bubbling and quetching of birds;
Of water gurgling
In gutters and chatter
And clatter of children
At break time over the wall;
And no doubt patter

Of insect legs drumming
Against twigs, in ricks
Of tickling straw
In this great appetite, this
Greedy maw
Called spring,
Calling for more, for everything
To be up and doing
Like me like me like me
The blue tit insists;
And in the evening
Before the dark comes down
Again with a bit
Of winter again
The blackbirds call
I am all yours
All yours, you-all.

Letter to comfort a friend

No, I don't like the rain either;
Nor can I stand the litter.
Nor the gross purple letters slurred
Across fine outlines, and proud memorials.
Martyrs, lovers, scholars held
You should not mind the sneers or stones,
The armies ruining the land,
The destruction of temples:
Their love the stronger for it.
The walls of the world
Have always oppressed the spirit;
Plastic detritus the thumbscrew, so,
These yobs – the wheel.

There are more accidents in the home than on the roads

I remember hearing a story of a whole family
Destroyed in one go by a ring of a doorbell.
No, not electrocution, nor gun shot.
Like this:

The young mother was bathing the baby when the bell rang;
The toddler hastening to answer, fell down the stairs
Skull cracked on arrival; the mother ran to the screams;
The baby drowned.
It was a telegram, the door, to tell her
Her husband had been killed in an accident.

Well, old friend, this was your Northern humour
To bring, to pantomime level, such Greek disaster
Told in such a way I could disbelieve it.
But I thought of that dreadful tale when I heard this one:

A disappointed girl waited at home
Long past the days when he might possibly ring
The first man who'd said he would.
Heavy-hearted, empty, she dragged upstairs
And then, wild buzzing, the phone was actually ringing.
Frenzied, she dashed, and gasping picked it up
Ready with her joy. 'Jane?' 'Oh yes!'
'Would you like to suck my cock? It's a great big huge one.'
Unlikely the stranger expected such blasts of tears.
Every time the phone rings she shakes with shame.

This day our daily...

How many times have I counted my blessings in the baker's,
How many times not grumbled because-it-doesn't-help-anyone-
       does-it? with the butcher,
How many times counted the five little cats watching from the hedge
Of the lady who sweeps her path, who also watches?
Whatever the weather has been
'Bit better today, i'n't it?' the newsagent says
Heart breaking.

Going to Sylvie's

The voice came loudly round the corner
'Now we're going to see Sylvie. Come along,'
Much louder than needed to instruct a child.
'What are you bringing me round here for, you see how I look
      after you,

I've got to follow your every step.
Just a minute here to please you then.
You see how gently I'm bringing you. You'll think of that.'
No lumbering idiot boy or old deaf person led,
The sturdy middle-aged back, not ill-clothed
Bent again to say, so we heard across the morning common
'Now we're going to Sylvie's. You'll see
That'll be nice. You really must come along now'
To a black dog.

High life

The daft things people do
Appal me.
Look at that woman, an island in the traffic
Clutching a terrified child by the hand; that is
No education at all. He
Is spued over by diesel fumes and all she
Does is stand him in it.

The daft things people do
Amaze me.
Could I be the sort of person to carry a huge umbrella,
Striped, on that narrow pavement?
That big man's in a daze; he
Doesn't care a bit if anyone else can live.

Fancy having three dinners in one week cooked for me.
If only I could keep up my intentions
Formed on rum and beer to be unwise, be
Careless and a tornado, prize the
Feckless and raucous and larger than life –
Striped umbrellas and silly women – then
I would
Surprise me.

If you can't join them beat them

I have finished with saying I'm sorry and waiting
While badly-driven sports cars cross my path
Their thin-lipped drivers glaring and shouting 'Fuck you!'
Nor do I lower my window now only to be harangued
By some yellow-eyed little runt who only knows
'You oughtn't to be on the road, you ought to be shot.'

I content myself by thinking how they'll wear their pants out
Stuck to their seats encased in their only armour,
Fish that must flop on land, legs useless as penguins',
And that the pulse in their ticking cheeks probably means
Apoplexy at forty.
I used to boil in silence under the shock.
Now I open up the throttle and yell back.

Modern witches 1: crouching

As I stir this soup my powers come back to me,
As I grind this powder and mix my special paste
And polish with fury my ceremonial bowl.
Outraged man with Rover you will be sorry
For what you shouted at the traffic lights:
My curses bring on the freezing shadow of age
Harden those disagreeable runnels in your face;
May the usual destructions that are coming to you
Hit you with more than ordinary pain.
And you, rude woman, throwing your weight on children
Your bus the only place you boss, rheumatics
Twist your jabbing fingers before age does;
May the drip forever dangle on your nose.
Pompous doctor showing off to students
Fish-moving mouth will one day never quite shut
And apoplexy silence who once squashed many;
Patronising dentist who tells lies
About drab patients' teeth, to get their fees
And leave town early Friday for golf with friends
(And midday Monday nurse tells moaning faces
'He is too busy, too busy, too greatly busy to see you')
May a nerve twitch in you no private practice

Can ever quell.
Pushers and shovers and sneerers and the square woman
Running the launderette for her chosen clients
(May you go round and round and up and down
And every time your squawking mouth shouts 'Help!'
Let floods of soap rush in)
All the things I couldn't say to you
Have boiled up now into this bitter brew.

Back in my dominion I devise remedies.

The powerless ever pretended to be witches.

Modern witches 2: sentinels

I know what you're doing, you figures standing at gates,
Straight pillars for legs, encased in bandages
Thick orange stockings fixed in turquoise slippers.
Your hair is screwed to yellow-whitey curls
Showing pink patches, and your lips tight clamped.
There are more of you behind the curtained windows.
You stand there for longer than to say good evening
To those who pass. As I move
Beneath the messages that cross the street
You are measuring my back, and getting details:
My haircut, jacket, gear, and the mates I go with.
You pretend you are looking down the road for your man
To put the potatoes on, but you are communing
With the other hags and warlocks in this road
To lay a curse and muck up our motorcycles.

Well, it's Friday night, and you wait till we roar round your corner.
That ought to smash your spells.

Just a snack for lunch

This do here, by the window? The steak's not bad.
– Yes, Elspeth, please, and a carafe of red I think.
Brought my friend Jack to see you, so do your best. –
The service is good here – foreign. There used to be

A smashing German. My God, what a bottom!
Mixed grill for you? Well, I'll have steak as usual.
Always do on Friday. It's steak tonight
And what my wife calls steak – well, you couldn't see it.
'Treat for you tonight, dear' she's going to say
'You work so hard. Two lovely days at home.'
And if I've had a fill-up at midday
I think of the plateful that I've had in here.
I close my eyes and sniff and smile at that.
She's very good, my wife. I don't know how
She manages the way she does. I'm grateful.
Thank God for the office grind and the lunch-hour rush.
Here comes the paté. Roll, Jack? Well, tuck in.

Visiting

We all go back with flowers
Well-fed, well rested.
Babies a year older
Wave bye-bye from all
The stations we stop at.

And yes, we will come again soon
To this upright life, these people:
Here we would recover.

Two minutes away from the station
The city throws its arms
Reflected in cafe doorways
Spilling on sleazy pavements
Music from lighted windows.
We sink to its solitudes.

Next time it will be the same
And the babies a year older.

Butcher's

White and silky neck with light brown curls
Soft like a calf's and a soft sparkly brown eye,
Will you in years become bristled and red –
Thick hanging neck of the slow-moving ox
The senior butcher you are learning from?
If you knew this, would you invite the axe
While you are still so young and palatable?

Sunripe

There are peaches, you know, and there are girls,
Girls who believed what their mothers told them
When they were talking to the clouds.

There are peaches, and there are people who eat peaches,
Sucking the juice, throwing the stone away.
Cannibals eat their enemies, not only for food
But to get their strength from the magic, from the blood.
Fruit eaters suck for the Good. Peach of a girl,
Glowing with all that a cannibal needs to revive him,
Peachy, take care.

Subscription

'Would you buy a flow-wer? Tenpence each for a flow-wer.'
Little gypsy girl who spoke so nicely
Why would I not buy a flower and let you think
You had something worth selling?
Certainly they were of value, your paper flowers.
I could have stuck it somewhere, and I'm sure
It would have looked pretty if I thought it did.
Who am I not to buy worthless things?
I've squandered far more than tenpence on bad beer
And not embarrassed. We are so canny now
So tasteful and sensible only the real sharks get us.
Little grimy trader next time I see you
I'll buy a flower.
But soon you will be indoors with all the might

Of modern expertise whirling around you –
That we have given rivers and fields away for –
Making plastic tops for rotten pens
As give-aways with packets of washing powder.
We crunch them in the gutter every day
In the very street where you were peddling flowers.

Little dots

Little dots on paper stand as a letter
And letters at a glimpse exhale a sound
Which to our habit represents a thing.
I put the squiggles and a world appears.
If I write 'numb' my toe hurts; 'lick' – there's a dog.

Down from this stair window, little dots
Are moving and changing in the space below.
They step, they turn, and, focused, take an aspect.
These flecks turn into persons that like clothes,
Put tins on shelves, itch, fancy themselves,
Suck at their teeth and think it terribly important
Which saucers to choose and whether the carpet's dirty.
On my table a man's photograph
Is looking at me with intelligence.
I pass my hand across. He is not there.
I touch a shoulder and I say a name
Only as someone tells me we say so.
Freed from the block of flesh the picture knows me
Because the life I've given him is mine.
I look in his eye and I see only my eye.
It has no blood from which the steam arising
Muzzes the head.
                          A squiggle slanting one way
Suggests a bosom, we lean a head against it.
Another line, a parrot in a pet shop
Shouting at its owner.
So we make rise a landscape from our breath
And set a shaft of sun slanting across
A chair, with a man in it outside his door,
His soft cloth slippers waggling from his feet.

Little pieces that I meant to show
Who jog and weave, wandering like firework sparks
Splinters of flak reflecting in the dark,
You swim in clusters as we peer about,
There are thousands of you flung upon the night
Each of you also trying to work out pictures
Of what that dark is made of.
And out there somewhere spinning on their own
The pet-shop man, the drunken friend, the pisser,
Neighbours, kind over walls, clacking advice,
Old woman in tweed coat and white summer straw
Helped by a man with horse's teeth, all gum,
Laughing as they cross the road, where stands
Sixteen-year-old Apollo, still sticky-mouthed
Gazing into a shop at his reflection.

I stand at the stairwell looking out on the plain.
The whisper has sunk. I cannot hear the voices.
What ghosts have conjured me, I wonder, to lap my blood,
And what will anchor, beyond my sight perhaps,
The kite string that keeps us flying? To make our world
We need the untrapped minute, unwriteable,
The real chrysanthemum that stinks and rots,
The breath of lips that mists the good clean mirror,
A hand on our shoulder, someone saying our name.

Lure

Someone a long way off is using my blood.
Maybe sip-sipping it when they lap the rain,
Maybe not getting the extra nourishment,
Maybe not tasting, in glasses they drink, the iron.

How have they siphoned it off and made it run
That way, without knowing it, without adjusting the lode?
Maybe some strength would return from that provendered flesh
If the face were to lift and show there, rising, my blood.

Veins that have used it pulse another way
The lymph that I need and they've taken is sluiced in the yard.

Some strong light has got itself into my brain
But instead of glowing, pulls, as a black cloth does,
The soft white filament that holds together my head
And vacuums, unneedy, the threads from their lodge in my mind.

On the far hill waves the luxuriant growth
Leaving this soil without its wanted food.

An instant on the viaduct

Moving at evening across the viaduct
On the regular train on ordinary business
The sun struck the side of the city before it sank
Leaving it flushed and softened when it had gone
And the bridge in the water fiery in the sunset.

The train stopped on the crossing, full, no doubt
Of cargo and equipment necessary
To provender the country, everything working
More or less well, wheels turning, people fed.
What if, I thought, I sprang from off this bridge
And floated into that tower that holds the light
Unmeshed by 'should' and 'next day' and 'your health'?

The sky shifted and crept back. The train moved.
I cannot leave it; not for nothing
I am commander of this Capitol.

I dare not leave, and yet I dare not not,
For out there is what feeds the city's power
That building I almost touch across the air
And far beyond the reach of such as I.

The dark curtained us in. I do not act.
I wait. The tower will topple anyway.

On the nature of scientific law

Newton watched a lot of balls
Flying through windows before he found
Beautiful in its general truth
The law that has no need of playthings –
Cricket bat lost, the apple long since rotten.

And so we move from rung to rung, or fall:
And get the view when our feet have left the ladder.
But I am attached to things, as a ladder to the ground.
I live off apples; the truth that climbs through me
Does not absorb the traces nor veil your face.

Figure in a landscape

A smell of burning like a noise erupts –
Doors slam and children chatter, wheel in, and fly
Off again like flocks of birds round fruit.
The machine hums and day turns out its thread.

Somewhere in this torrent is a place
Within the fall where a drop of water hearkens
Slowly on its own in the cave of water;
Takes the surroundings in and from its surface,
Tensed and unbroken, gives back the white spray rising.

The smashed cascade tumbles with fragments of day;
Somewhere you cannot touch behind the roaring
The coiling rope twists as one stream of water.

Somewhere within the house is a chamber of air
Where clearly, when you are gone, I see and hear you;
Where everything that I say perfects my sentence,
Where everything that you hear was my aim to say –
Each movement and outline remaining always the person.

But what we say through doors and on stairs, real
In a different way when bodies really stand there
Blurs the mirror with its actual breath.

A man's feet planted at the water's edge
Will join the mirrored body in the river:
Mirror of eyes produces the land within
The gazer's eyes, not rooted in outward objects.
The foil of my mind peels back when you are here
And your image plunges into the darkness there.

FROM **BEYOND DESCARTES**
(1983)

Back to base

Mole who knows
Who burrows up for air
Sniffs, intoxicated, so much fresh stuff:
River smell, green of leaves; sniffs space
Feels (heady) the air, feels space swirl round,
Senses (he cannot see) that stars beyond
Beyond what he could ever want or think of
Reel and hold sway behind the dark up there.
That dark is far enough – a thin dark
Not like his, familiar, close to pelt
Holding him.

And mole returning in time before the world swoops
Perhaps a little after the point danger might come
And the light break and trap him and bludgeon him;
Mole missing the ether, creeps to his place:
Close corridors he does not need to see.
Weeps for the stars and space and fresh green smell
The river moving by mysteriously
He does not know, but knows something is there
Stream where others flourish, that others can use,
Weeps but how comforting the smell of earth
How truly right his own dark; basement
Where the bend
Cuts out the ruinous light
The brittle noises, laughter of thundering horses
And suchlike hysterical creatures.
Round the next bend, and the low breathing
Of his own life and all his life around him
Imperceptible in the upper air, receives him
Concentrated positive and tangible.
Mole he sleeps deep, his velvet nurtured by
The proper dryness, cohesion, in the earth
His only place, he knows,
Safe from the pull of the malign dews of the stars
The vast cold glitter, thin twanging in the spheres
That draws men, crazy, across shadeless tundra.

Descartes – you there?

Here we are, I drink to you:
The World, the liquor in this glass
Window reflection in this amber
The Upside-down Beyonds that pass.

The world is only in our sight
As instance this reflection here.
I know the roof goes on the top
But in my glass the houses stop
Half-way down, and, chimney-first
Plunge into the sky.
Where solid frozen ground should be
The streaks of sunset lie.

Put down the glass, or drink the drink
Or merely turn your head away
And once again the top is top
And houses grow up from the earth
And that's the way they stay.

So must we disbelieve our sense
Which after all is all that I
Have to test consciousness against?
And how long should we watch and wait
In a swinging world to say that now
Is the Now to hold to, come what may?
And then which sense do we believe:
The one where wine is in the glass
(The lip untouched, unclouded mind)
Or, glass now clear, wine drunk, the one
That thinks it sees things straight?

Knock knock

Here in this picture on the mantelpiece
You see Grandpapa and Grandmama,
She sitting, writing; he standing behind her chair
Hand gently on satin shoulder of long-sleeved dress.

So begins the poem; but – who knows? –
They may have been actors in an Ibsen play;
Or, less substantial, but just as needed
The image in a lonely person's head
Reaching across a table late at night,
That it would have been nice so to have stood, have leant
To have a family, and grandparents worth preserving
Living in a house of substance in Darwin's Cambridge.

I hear the door go, blink my eyes, and he's gone
My man in his study dreaming up a world.
Reader, do you so dream me? To write this down
I must imagine me here pen in hand,
Back of an old envelope, running feet, knock,
Knock, 'will dinner be ready soon?'
                                    There is
No dinner, no stairs, no room or pen and paper
If you – Are you there Reader? – do not read and make one.

And when I sit in your room, dear, and you reach across
To get a paper to show me something, have I
By looking forward lost you in the present,
Or having made you, understand you better
Than ever happens in raw life outside?
These mirrored mirrors lead us nowhere fast.
Solitary reader at night that I have conjured
Reaching across to pick up a picture that you
Imagined yourself into, turn round again.
Step out of the frame that I have trapped us in
Place your hand on my shoulder and take away the pen.

Abstract study – circles

I stand again on the shore
Where we stood and watched the waves.
Or rather, since I write this
I imagine us standing there.

So I sit, town-girt, and imagine
Me standing by you on the shore
But the vision not being a pen
Me writing was only a thought.

I was walking around the streets
Busy, and the mind moving
And now that I sit at my desk
Holding an actual pen
I remember the pleasant morning
When I saw myself sitting down
Late on a warm evening
And fixing this scene of something
That now is so tiny and far
So painted, so set and silent
In the glass of the inner eye

That the only thing left to do
Is to take you by the hand
And run up the bank to the sea,
And

I sit here making up that.

Not a rootless lily

'The island! That mark, South Bay; look– ' 'Yes,
And that dirty smudge, the trees;'
'This bit here – here, give's a pencil. There
That's where the jetty was and the other side – '
'We never saw the house till the woodland burnt
That night she wouldn't let the firemen on.
Did you believe she *was* mad, like they said?'

'Dunno. Don't throw it away. The place to a T.
The way it seemed to float, a blotch in your eye
You thought was the strain of staring, or seaweed; then suddenly
Stepped forward, clear, out of the mist upon you.'

A scrumpled bit of paper, a boot's heel-mark,
An idle moment holding off the day
Letting in other times, as a breeze pushes
Thick drapes of air to let show, solid and brown
Land under sunshine sleeping on the water.

Who has not run up steps and knocked on a door,
Head tilted up to see a head at a window
Blown out, twenty years since, where now thin air
Stretches above a playground; who has not walked
Into the arms of long-departed friends?

It is a cliché, old in Shakespeare's time,
That things made out of nothing, mists and breaths
Like fever fumes will fill our minds until
That city is solider to our witched selves
Than the vague earth we stand on.
                                    Master, they say
Your power is made of words, without your book
All air – nothing, that is; and that your island
Was only a pattern of the mind, a symbol
For what art is; that we're trapped forever
In our brain's fashioned pool.
Not art, but being human, we no way
Can not be mused by spells; the air as full
Of apparitions as the isle of noises.

But Prospero made his tempest to get his daughter
Back to the mainland, and himself set free;
Surely there must have been, to conjure one,
Somewhere an island we have scrambled on,
Surely, to body Miranda's dream, some kiss?

Bound upon a wheel

Let me try again. I look
At the same fence as before, at a tree
Whose leaves I tried to fix last time. I say
It looks this way this time because it's August
And the heavy sky diffuses all the light
So generally, we feel that it is dead.
We sense the thin leaves, understand the season.

And I say it looks like this because my light
Has gone, for the time being, because sap
Down at the bottom has no strength to move
The lively yellow leaves to catch the light
And make me think of sunbeam.

I say this view is here assembled only
By a mind not made of trees, bricks, fibres or fences
Window-frames or birds or chimney-pots
Willow-herb or petrol-cans on roofs
Or roofs even.
I say that on another day these things
Will seem different and that other people
Running in with fresh faces must see it new
And I will raise my head and from their eyes
Taking the glimmer say I see it too.

But I know
Whatever veils the turning year may cast
We all come back to this: running, running
Only to stand still.
                    Come, do we need,
Now that the window is emptied, to look any more
On these scenery flats used for any old show?
Must the bright limbs of others drag this ground
To get to the same point which again is nowhere:
Three trees of the magic wood, then into cold wings
Blocked asbestos fire-door to a blank brick alley?

And even this has been thought again and again.

Yet I am held, and I am held by things.
The cabbage white
Flapping like every other nemesis
Has only ever done that; to be cabbage white
Must do it still. Only by doing again
Each done thing do we live a minute – you stop and you die.
We must run to stand, and to keep the tree
Must try to see it still, with no let-up
Like breathing every minute keep the contract.
So I am drawn to the window, so I must look
Must see me looking and –

This is an old story
And me telling it is an old story.
I have been here before. I did not leave
It will not change. And so I turn away
I will not look. This is a trick to keep me
Poor blind donkey plodding the road and so –
And as I turn away, surely a brightening
Surely a strengthening behind the houses
A stirring in the light, a shifting – for see:
Diaphanous the leaves, some yellow on them
Moving like butterflies, see, it is all lifting
The air is dancing and – You fool. You fool!

False postulate

A flock of seagulls on a field –
'Oh that means storms at the coast,' I said.
'You've got it wrong' as you shook your head,
'They live on the lakes. They are always here.'

What other essential wisdom have
I based on misinformation
And, unaware of deformation,
Leaned on a world that isn't there

But floats some feet above the earth
Rooted in supposition;
Based on premise not on stone,
Separate, complete; like a bubble of air?

And if, because I like your hat
Or eyes, or because the shape of your hand
Reminds me of people I have loved,
I take as fact that you understand

I find myself in this muddy field
As the winter light sinks in the ground
And strange birds with no tidy story
Lurch in circles closer round

With love and its signs as miles apart
As pigeon-seagulls and the sea;
Meaning and manifestation
Knotted far away from me

In bright rooms where the people greet
Things and facts they know they know;
And I across this weary field
The long way homeward plodding go.

Living off other people – Welfare

It would be pretty to have roses
Flourishing by my back door.
It would be nice to have a well-kept house
With velvet chairs not scraping a polished floor.
It would be lovely to sit down at dinner
Grey tie, pearl pin, fresh shirt and well-kept hands
And good to have a purring car in a clean garage
Eye-catching as the best brass bands.

But to keep it all going would be a lot of worry
And anyone who does it has to race and scurry
Seeing to roofs and pruning, maintenance and mechanics,
A shower of rain, a little green fly, bring on terrible panics
And ruin and failure shadow every path.

So I think this is the best thing to do:
As I walk down roads I see so many flowers
Nod-nodding in all the gardens that I pass.
I can glance into other people's rooms that they have furnished
And look how courteously that man is turning
To open the front door to his gleaming house.
Did you see how his suit fitted him, his perfect cuffs? Spotless cars
Slide by with women in furs and perfumes
Wafted to me with the flavour of cigars.

I am wrapped in my layers of shapeless coats
And I need never polish or dig or set
The table out for four distinguished guests
Or get to an office or prove myself each day
To provide for hammocks and lawns,
To get my antiques protected against insects.
A guest everywhere, I look in as dinner is served.
As I tramp past others' gardens, the rose opens.

Derivations

Translation

It is no answer
To call with others' voices;
To wear their shoes
To paint their pictures.

This is our town
Our grit, our yobbos, we tussle
Hate breathed in living faces,
These black jackets open.

Dante's concretion
For us is pearl, enlightening.
Here now, the grit
Our oyster has it.

Geranium

Out of the cellar, scraping around for coal,
I drag a pot with a root in it, shoved there
In muddled days before frost. Undeserved
This sudden switching on of waiting leaves.
Almost like mould, so stuck on they seem to be
Atopic on a dead old bit of twig.
With perfect competence the green rag breathes.
A young man writes to me that it is spring.

Cherry

Suddenly the cherry has opened.
I could pretend it was love
Like the babe opening its eye.

Twig thickening on the air
Has become this burst of blossom.

It waves its appeal in the spring breezes;
O cherry, O open heart.

Story

Off she goes, my little Red-Riding-Hood
Cased in jeans, cheeky, with smiles and joy
To see her Gran.
Oh, wolf, be friendly.
She thinks she is tough enough
To eat you up – irresistibility
(How can she not be? She thinks she's the cat's whiskers)
Itself.
Couldn't you, just for once, stay away wolf.

Watching a child watching a witch

Don't think it won't come to you:
Groping in bags on the pavement outside the shop
Tipping everything out to desperately find
The three-times-replaced purse, key, glove.

But think this also:
She may once have been, as now you are,
An image of youth, a sweet fresh hopeful
Stamped on some old haggish wandering gaze.

Lady

Poor twisted lady, what can the world seem like
With those great sideways-knocking hoofs
And long neck bobbing?

Much the same as to you, ducks – handsome lad:
Sometimes calm and lovely, sometimes mad;
Same difference.

X marks the spot. A postcard from home

Lit the fire last night.
Wished you were here;
Stared into the glowing coals;
Thought of you, dear.

Good stretched alone by the fire
Thinking, dear
Nicer things, very likely
Than if you'd been here.

There's the post come.
Nothing from you, dear,
Telling me what you've done
Wishing me there.

Even in the magic fire
Images cool, dear
Come again so I may think that I
Wish you were here.

Cloud

Summer cloud
Seeming to pause, seeming to look at yourself
Summer cloud, you trail across the lake
Breaths and fragrances of your journeys:
Orchards a thousand miles away that now
Hang cherry-thick for birds, like a star
Sending light out of time, you bring
Past season's blossom to this passing minute
Expanding it
As yourself before distillation.

You have passed my love lying in the meadow
And my love's love, and brought their honey with you;
And the bee's zuzz from some lily throat
We shall never throttle, you encase in this silence.

I would say, dower it all on this sweet home meadow
Pasture braked by trees, quiet encircled;
Let drowse here concoction of your exotic gatherings
Let me taste your world.

But you, who are nothing when not a mirror
Drift on, vaguely changing to take on all comers.

Well, summer cloud,
Take my thoughts with you then.

Moon

Cold moonlight
Is it you stopping my marrow seeds from growing?
Is it you who keep away my friends?
Jealousy, jealousy
It will do you no good to lure me to the cliff
For then I shall spot the fraudulence of your attraction
Broken in the black waves;
And as I fall I shall curse you with bitter breath.
That is no way to get me, little to love in that.
Leave go, moonlight
Return me.

Rose

Rash flower
Gazing, now you have topped the wall
Staring into this sequestered garden
What can you bring from the outside world
What of frenzy
What of dancing
What fire in the veins of the earth that sets you blazing
Above this windless garden,
Rash flower?

Still reading fairy stories

If you were bred on fairy tales
As was I
You would know where the prince was going to
And why;
And if you had then also lived in the world
As I have done
You would know too that he went past the ten-foot wall of roses
And kept straight on.

And if I told you that somehow he once turned back
And hacked his way through
Would you join in then, and finish the story the way
I wanted you to;
Saying that the clash of light when she woke was
Cymbals of bliss
And the power of life through that long-waiting silence was
All in the kiss;

And agree, since we lounge in the court of a great castle with a
        hundred years' sign
That says: 'For Sale'
It must be that we are bewitched, and that this is
A fairy tale.

The feast

We saw this beautiful confection in the window
Castled and cherried and glazed with dazzling white
Hard as snow crust. Signalled to by delight
We crossed the road. You wanted it for me.

So I, drawing on magic then, planned how, for pleasure
Taking it, I would both have and serve it
For you to eat entire and yet preserve it.
And I went home to summon up a feast.

Then you thought, perhaps it was too much,
Too rich and too bizarre to suit your taste.
And the trimmings on the box were such a waste!
You brought assorted goodies in its stead.

And piled them up into the space I'd made
For the absent astounding centre-piece. Why,
I thought, had I bothered? You kept the ribbon by –
It might come handy for another time.

Having sat and seen the spread all ready
You thought perhaps we'd do without the fruit
On the pudding. It made it difficult to cut.
Absent-minded, you picked at a rim of icing

And turned it round to hide the gap from me.
Then with a flourish set down on a plate
A nice large slice indeed. But I could not eat:
The food looked cardboard-dry and tampered with.

And all the picnic seemed unsavoury
Bites out of little pies scattered in the sun
Halves of withering sandwiches, and everyone
Suddenly with his mind and needs elsewhere.

You moved off fast. You did not stay to clear.
And passing that same window happened to see
(And thought how so much luckier was he)
Who'd got that cake to cut into and swallow

Great luscious mouthfuls, teeth sinking through the icing
(And how you really should have had a share).
You spoilt what was on offer with your care
And self-regard. And so you lost it all.

That magic cake – you could have had it whole.

Puppeteer

At Christmas time
Men make these little boxes lined with velvet
And put on magic shows
And each small lady fits exquisitely
The measures planned for her to gravely dance through
And each cravatted beau holds out his hand.

Cross-legged on carpet
In velvet party-dresses clean soft children
Gaze through their shining curls.
The masks he's made seem like real skin that moves
In grief and joy, more than in the windy
Empty grey streets. And all follow his story.

It is a delight
Grown-ups in the room would live, with the heavy red hangings
Hiding the picture-window.
'He is so clever with bits of wood and cloth
You'd think he'd tamed them with his leads of cotton.
See how they bend according to his story.'

The bleak slopes wait behind the dark, outside,
That is blotted out by means of thick red cloth
From those in whose arteries something sways and tells
That it is Christmas time.
We would not survive out there, O puppeteer
Nor your charmed audience. But can you wonder
That in another season when the ice
Cracks, and the avalanches grumble, and something moves
So that through the cracks pale fronds can come
And into the air the songs of birds and water,
Can you wonder in another season –
Your smile cracking –
The puppets shall turn over and refuse
Saying:
'The wolves and mountain whirlwinds would not suit you
Since only puppets satisfy you now.
Go back into your box and wait for us.
We only work this show at Christmas time.'

129

Another old tale

One small soldier going towards the mountain
'Ho, ho' shouting; 'I am not one to lurk
Waiting for the beast to kill me.
No; out and after it, trample its lair, push to its core.
That's my system.
Thus I am out from the last tight circle of corn
That shivers in the razed field, packed with fear
Great eyes between every stalk attracting death.
I am out and away before the beaters come,
Half-way to rifling their homestead.'

With flask, exercises, pemmy, courage up
Expert in preparation, custom-built equipment,
Off he goes, to fight winter.
Through the storm he came, across the tundra
With never a tree, never a stake to support him.
The sun came out and sparkled on the snow.
'How right I was, see now' he breathed his song
And his own vapour on the air entranced him.
'The fight is to the brave. Come on. I prosper.'
He marched on, breathing rare air, using his substance.

Through the slow ages two white ears of glacier
Peered on the rim of the mountain six miles sheer
A bowl on the top of the sky,
Animal-intent, it paused, caught
By the tiny creeping movement across the plain
Drawing within its circle.

He used his food up in three days; in six
His skins were tattered; the everlasting rocks
Held thousands of years of ice packed in this present
And thousands yet to go.

Whistling, as he knew how, to let himself know
His lungs were in good shape, caring for his feet
He hardly had time to see where the sky's maelstrom
Opened and came down, the point where black and white
Meet in an extreme of blindness, itself blanked out
By the whirling *néant* exhaustless in its powering.

As of a vague white paw the abyss hit him
A cream-coloured tiger's cuff, absent-minded,
The pit of its eye swivelled on a far horizon.

The edge of a fly-wing mashed into the rock
Half-way down through this orb, has not less substance
Than this little speck of grit, propelled a half-inch
Dreaming a state called summer, a world thought human.

Untitled

Every year when the extreme cold
Falls suddenly over us, cracking the skin
Straightaway, that has been oiled by summer,
Freezing to a standstill the heart, strangling movement,
I hear the same awful story, in different versions.

I had begun to think it was the myth-making faculty
Like the wartime story that a man in Australia
And a man in Finland
Heard from his father:
The limb blown off that landed in his dinner
In the exact same way; and only some detail revealed
(A sock in one version, in another a hand with a mitten
In one a lamb chop, in another a plate of porridge)
That this was a variant of archetypal legend
And brought relief and laughter that it was not real.

An idiot brother chained to a bed for years;
The drunken return only to punch up the wife,
Every year pregnant, and to get her pay-packet;
Dog on cushions and relative in a boxroom
Kept on biscuits.
Punch hitting Judy over the head with a stick.

                        Gruesome stories
Arising, miasma from marshes, from the foetid pools
That stand in the human mind.

Alas not so, alas I am forced to listen:
They found a child of eight dead in a bath.
It had been a night, the coldest over Christmas
When – heating in the house, good dinner inside me
Woolly scarf round my feet, five blankets, thick mattress
Eiderdown, bottle – I had felt too freezing
To put out my arm from underneath the bedclothes
The air inside the house had such a bite.

The child had nothing on, there was no towel
No flannel he could clutch or put against him.

The window had been wedged open and the door locked.
The snow-laden wind cut through the curtainless room
Keeping the enamel five degrees below freezing.

The child was frozen blue in the empty white bath
His urine an iced runnel.

It was Christmas Eve when his parents locked him in.

This year I hear that last night there in Poland
It was 37 degrees below and men
Taken across the snow-stormed plain, were made
To stand outside the wagons in the dark
And hosed down with water that instantly froze on them
And left till dawn, standing in ice-bound Europe.

Who are these people? The woman I see in the grocer's
Polite to customers? The couple who, arm in arm
Every Saturday morning go to the Post Office?
Numbed, as with cold, all I do is mouth
In a silent howl, like the paralysing frost,
'How long – – ? How long?'

Another year; a summer has intervened,
A healthy fat baby next door is leaping about.
A little chill breath of autumn creeps through the dusk.
I close the back door, think about lighting fires.
Tired, a bit cold, I think of an early night:
Some warm food, a bath and a soft clean blanket – and sleep.

In my hot bath lies drowned the ice-dead child.

In memory of God

I suppose they would've shot the moon down,
If they could have, into little pieces,
To make a new one
Even while saying isn't it strange, isn't it beautiful.

Come, I will show you a marvel
Of man.

There on the green
A huge contraption in a palisade.
'You have here a perfect replica of a whale.
Every branch of knowledge known to man
(You name it, we got it) has gone into this project
To bring you the fabulous wonders of the deep.'

Yes, here's a panel
That tells you who gave grants for what to whom
And who the electrician was, and which boroughs
Raised a penny rate to send the team
To find the stuff to make the eyes – et cetera.
'Ask him not to touch, lady, would you mind? –
Just to look at, son, so you know what they looked like –
We need a grant for a pool, and another two thou to get it
Buoyant, so it would *move*. Then there's maintenance.'

Far in perpetual waters a creature turned
Coasted and turned in perfect machinations
Moving, like clouds at the edge of the world, untended
Simply itself in its extraordinary being:
Easy, so easy moving through the water.

Stupid men. All you had to do
To get a whale, was not to spend one penny, not do anything
But let be what miraculously was there.

No one on earth can make a whale again.
And when, because of what you have made way for
The rats over-run us, think of the mild wonders
We could have let keep the world:

Unclever, not like us, yet much more skilful
And useful, alas, in all their parts to man.

But being no use would probably not have saved you:
The strange shining disc that lights you to your extinction
Far over your dark pathways,
And even whatever caused the moon's pull, the life of waters
To maintain the whale –
They would put it in their pocket if they could.

Shadows coming

From the derelict garden creeps the cat;
And spirits; and thoughts.
Wild – all.
During the day the garden had stood back
A place to walk past, street-sober,
Unremarkable.

How has it held what for so long I have not thought of
This shadow that surrounds nowhere I have seen?
Why does this place I have never set foot in and shall not
Ooze out on the night air something of what I have been?

Traveller, you think you have gone far.
You have learnt to pack, travel light, full of expertise
To hold to the road, to be lucky, avoid plague towns;
And one dusk you may, inadvertent, pass a place, a bit of air

And from it will seize
You in the gut the feral eye-beam of the animal,
Old thoughts you thought swallowed and passed;
And the spirits, for some time shrunk and tamed, once again
Wild – all.

Beyond Descartes

Look at the wall, she said
See where the bricks join together
Glowing fire-soft, sheen of dove-breast
Shop-silk purple slashed into matt pit brick,
Crumbling kiln-yellow

Look at the wall and watch where I go, she said.

Not dream. Clarity more than daylight
Clarity of the long slow stare.
And I tried to follow, be where the voice led
Taken in with it as it moved away
Through the wall.

Came slap up against it, grazing me.
Beating with open palm 'oh oh' on the rough flat side
No edge, no crevice for purchase, no way round
No way except back, hurt, ricked (body still onward against it)
To see where the great slab stood
Brick side of the ordinary house that was there next door.

The tree crashed and brought the sun down with it
Flaming its net of branches;
Its reared roots tumbled the wall.
No secret chamber there, only wide waste
No courtyard with its birdsong almond tree
No lifted latch on the warm waiting kitchen
No velveted and fragrant sitting room
Just a wide waste of rubbish on a dump.

* * *

Christmas Eve
And each must pull the fabric where he can
To shield him.   You, of course
Beyond the wall, beyond my speech, within
The jagged fingers of the storm, lying
In the blue airless centre, the still eye.

O fever friend, why did you let me go?
What else but thick dark air, now, and flat drab fields?

Christmas Eve
Figures scurry in dark afternoon
Wrapped in the weeping weather
They do not burn my fingers when I touch
Partial, hopeless, human; and sometimes the smile
The sudden gift of a face from within its claddings
Lifted in some sort of love or need, but lifted from
Such ugliness, such lack of will, such grudging.
Habitat: stained concrete, broken things
Plastic-tangled corners where they stand
Stuffing their mouths and shitting.
More like an animal's cage, who sullen, stuck
Lets fall the peel and drools the pith from its mouth
Not moving, not shaking the messings from its skin.
Flies cluster at the eyes and are not brushed off
And this in freedom not in captivity.

Men more than animals   foul their lair
Slut puppets suffocate in greed's dun leavings.

Well, were I spirit, were I Shelley, were
I absolute for life, I could maintain
My hand unshrivelled in your scorching fire
And absolute for death would then become,
Here, where it rains, and the earth softens to mud;
And so could stand
And let these appalling waves flow over me
Safe in my box within;
But, human, need the human hope, and hope
Leaves us agasp at what the human is.
Shall we consign the world to rot, and leave – for where?
The golden tower of our fantasy?
The pretty flower that chances out of mud?
Brave smile, the courage, stupendous energy
"In face of ", "against odds", the pale soft beams
Broken, of human love, across the vast
Wreckage of foul flood water –
Heart-emptying actions, springing useless tears?

Frail barque to carry courage in, poor raft
Tossed in three-mile waves: the struggling smile
Against fang anger, calmness occasionally heard,
The man who perhaps by chance might one time walk
Across a town to take a wallet back
For no convenience that is his.
                                    The waves
Race through the night continuously around
The black and howling Pole; the pale cold sun
Struggles through dowsing clouds enough to show
The shipwreck of a splintered raft, frail barque.

Oh we pin it exactly, get to the root,
I see, I understand. Compassion spreads.
I net the meaning and polish a stone of it
Essence   and the boil lanced.
And out there not one inch less of water
Not one rat the less scavenger the less
Drowned. No small scratch altered
On any child's knee.   Not one more
Trembling old man got across
To the other side of the road from where he was waiting
Not one gratuitous curse and bottle thrown the less.

In the slow dropping rain I seek some grace
Goodness, ordinary, within the pale,
Spotty, blotched, dull, but sending on its way
The patched-up body, and the skin grows over,
Some action at least – to put out a hand is service –
Something that helps more than the path of flame;
Soft earth, soft sullied beasts perhaps in this close air
Where the glory on the rock gets not one muscle moving.

And this is what I see:
A cripple crossing a road to save a dog
Kicked in fair gardens not frost destroys but sullen
Dirty well-fed men carve up with knives
That people sit in factories to make –
Precision and expensive, care and thought taken.
As if all good
Were only an opposition in face of danger
A shaft brought out to highlight the cloud, and then

Ever a fading;
Floppy brief petal that falls away for a fruit
Hard, bitter, and the death of the plant, shrivelled
In ill-will's energy.

Christmas Eve morning – a paradox of words
But no bells, no clangour, no concourse, no celebration
Even the tinsel and such marks as there were
Is rubbish only now, to be cleared; nuisance,
Litter and drunks far flung.

Salvation through human love and sacrifice
A dead idea, and one that works in practice
Only in very limited circumstances
That do not have a bearing on these people.

* * *

Back across the gulf to my habitation
A bleak wind, blowing out of everything
Colour, all gleam, leaving shoddy, lustreless
Skin and other cheap wrappings, lumpish faces.
The grit loaded the air round these Saturday shoppers
Dragging dull bags of goodies that did not cheer them
Ash on the tongue.
We had got round, I realised, to the days
That should have been spring.

I came into the room: tired, closed
To effort, conversation, thought. Small tasks
All I was fit for and so began,
Sullen like them, what was close to my hand.
In the course of which my neck naturally moved
And there the wall
That I had gone away from, that had blotted –
As an urgent dream evaporates into the day –
Stood.   But so shining
So full of mica, black and crumbling red
Palpitating like fire, oscillating with myriads
Of tiny explosions – dandelion seeds, or midges, or the spots
That swim past tired eyes, floating but held
Within some frame of vision.

Whitsun, I thought, and yesterday the cold hard wind:
Abasing, sweeping clean, taking every morsel
Of human will that says 'I am' and 'therefore',
Whirling up with the litter man-made constructions
Of how the world should be, of what man should have,
A shrivelling ash wind from a dark cold sky
But scouring to make ready
To receive – ? what? –
           Breath of the spirit? Bride of whiteness? holy ghost?

Back across the gulf of my habitation
To find in the dusk the wall shining in the rain
A bird singing from its chimney-pot
Or somewhere in an upper air, sending
News of space, of soaring, apprehension
Of something moving there not bird or wall,
And some sort of voice calling, or hardly heard
Railway trucks' thin noise at night that wakes you
To sound of violins, you could believe
Music of spheres, small metal harmonies;
Or ordinary bird that, in half-wakefulness
Has poured a legendary song, quicksilver
Gone before seized, but leaving in its wake
Marvel of pure air, the first breath
Of blossom in the world, like the white bird whose singing
Could restore sight to the blind.

Bird of my spirit, where are your lifting wings?
Song of my mind   clear your lovely voice.

As a dog moves along a track of unheard whistle
I leant to the line of sound with all my attention
Holding to that thread with my senses as feet do a hill.
Look at the wall and listen to the air it said
Come
Now or not.
            Farewell you
Walls of the world   guided by its going
I follow.

The inland sea

Did I tell you of a strange dream I had?
I was in the upper country, mule country,
The track twisting, dust, stone; sometimes,
Standing rare and beautiful, a thistle
On a cliff edge. White sky behind it.

Suddenly, singing
Was coming up the valley; and as it neared –
The little group, you could see that it travelled with them –
The green carpet of the valley floor:
Grasses and fronds with hanging heads, and mosses.

The fore man stood by me on the cliff
A Chinese ivory sage that fits in the palm
With every thousand hair in his beard distinct
And wrinkles lining a face as smooth as a pebble
But complete and whole; and this man spoke to me.

'It is the inland sea we seek,' he said
'And we will journey ever,' and round the mountain,
As they moved on like a shoal in the ravine bottom,
Winding as one, like a cloud across the sky,
Their distant singing swayed and ebbed with the wind
And I felt safe because these old men sought
The inland sea.

I remember a girl telling me
(Brown curly hair, fresh skin and open eyes
Sweet honest and innocent English abroad –
I don't think they are made like that any more –)
Of her meeting the man that she was now engaged to.
They had met and she dreamt that she was married to him
And the second time she saw him told him her dream.
She was not bold or fishing or plotting consequence
'Wasn't it strange' she'd said 'to have such a dream?'
And he asked her to marry him.

Why do I, a life time late, these years after
Talk of dreams, fabricating premises
When we both know it may be so or no
And not matter; when the direct truth
And the direct lie are mudded by convenience
And compromised;
When all is a game we would like to win, but know
The losing will shake us for only a little while
Before we slip back into our haze of self
Where all is slumber within wired-up walls?

Why? Listen. Come a little closer, near as you dare
To the edge of this spur. The soil's a little crumbly
But there are hawthorns, sloes and other bushes
Knitting the escarpment. Here is shade
And safety on the edge of danger. A place I found
By long trekking, retreating at times with care
Not to loosen rock, and going about
Another way until I found this nest.
Listen. Inch forward. What do you hear in the wind
That, freed from the bluffs, is meandering with the river?
Look up to the sky an instant, do you not see
Immense lakes of light lying within the clouds?
Part these grasses: spread out fair below
The hidden, ancient, still-fructifying source
Silent shines in sunlight.
Can you see? Come a bit nearer then. Now.
Look: we have come to the inland sea.

Man as matter

Man as matter
(ISLAND; PHYSICS)

There is the mirror and in it the pale dawn.
The light that strikes it is the light that lifts us;
And from your face I say 'give me the world,
Give me the heat and power that through your eyes
Acts as a burning glass to fuel this island.'

But if I grasp the mirror the dawn disperses
Fading back to the sky like exhalations:
Through unconfining air it thins, it rises;
And over the long day I must go collecting
Splashes of light painted on trees, on houses.

The neck of glass kicked from the path of the sun
Dynamos nothing; dingy bottle-bit
Harmful only, blood letting, no valour in it.

The vigours of day strike, pulsate, expire.
We may be there or not, can only admire.
You, like a piece of physics generate
With no connection beams from a dead star.

Man as image
(MASSIF; CHEMISTRY)

Imagine a black lake
And out of the mountains comes, by chance, a figure.
After years, the traveller through the massif
Comes on this pool. By extreme chance he struck it:
The only opening he could break into
This circle of space, escaped from the hooded upland.

And cannot believe, after this luck, this reach,
That no sweet water strikes adown a valley
Tracking a footway out of choked moraine
And flank on flank of cliff heaving to the horizon.

And cannot at first take in that the figure there
Seeming to sit on the other side of the tarn
Was shadow only
Shadow on a surface
Circular, colourless, thick as oil, and breathless.

                              but bowed his head
As if the only way his face could know
That other face, was looking in the pool.

Deep in black water turning, moving, yearning
The figure he sees – oh is it drowning, sliding
Or clouding and blotting as sky trails do
Made, as they are, of nothing?
The stone has sat there for a million years
Making that outline when the light is so.

If he does not move, the man will die.
Transfixed with loss, he sways on up the scree
Shocked, clutching at rubble, sick with grief.
The air comes back into his blood containing
The turn of a head, the memory of a meeting.

Man as cannibal
(PLAIN; BIOLOGY)

A man in four blank walls will wither away
Eyes starved, no changeful air upon his skin
His ear sealed by the pressure of no stir
Upon the drum that beats into his brain.

The roofer's tapping through the mist brings in
Chatter of birds, far waters, the sound of the sea.
Soup of the air feeds us; it is honey-combed
With channels of movement that lap and oil life back
To the blanched body through its desiccation.

But a man cannot live from breezes round a rock
Or shapes in a cloud.
Stone does not feed upon another stone
But a man a man;

A plant, though lined with minerals, the same.
A man must gobble if he wants to breathe
And what flesh is there that is not his own?

Look at a field of cabbages in the empty
Wintry Eastern counties left alone.
The light from the sky falls on them; and if anyone
Were there to look, they would see such light
Gleam from these as from the tight head of a child.

See what has blossomed! Could you not curl your tongue
And draw it down, this soft flax butter skin
Hay fragrance of the sleeping child, tow-haired young man
With milky throat; as cows munch chrysanthemums,
Breathe on and lick, the bear and its hungry young?

The fleeting antelope rouses the cheetah. One leap
Fixes it in its entrails; it nuzzles, it grips,
Timed to the pulse it laps up for its feeding.

Man to live must get his teeth in flesh,
Tastiness oozing round his itching canines,
Aroma and sweet slap of roast on tongue,
Ichor, saliva mlngling, palate to throat
And down to the gnaw in the pit; and we move, we grow
We reach our arms in vigour, thick hair in a sheen
Lies on the pillow, linen crisp and fresh:
Pap, flesh; renewing what the man lets fall,
Uses, evaporates or wears away
And sets him there to gulp another morning.

For all his champing he is not assuaged.
Some fire in the gut has burned it all away.

He goes to visit in her high room as would be
The young deer moving softly in her skin.
White room with velvet cushions, red velvet dress
Plum-bloomed furry clothing over flesh that ripples
Satiny with winks of life.
'I need, I leech; – and then all ashy lies
The source of light, the life-shiner, the dancer.
Dim, then, the room, exhausted the husk, the rags;

146

No fulling to them; flabby are the veins
Dried blood, cracked eyes, fit only for scavengers.'

Not enough, he says, not that meal.
Some draught in my back, some thin place in my shoulder
Leaves me vulnerable; perpetual shiver.
Your bone-case drawn round me, I would be safe,
Curled in warm streams, caved in your wall of mountain
Lodged in your blood and bones, I move with you.
You'd make the effort, I be supplied with it.

And see the healthy bursting prosperous man
His muscled leg pushing the earth down.
It is not beef supplies but, circling his veins
The lymph he pumps through her incestuous system.
No wonder they thought up the body and blood of Christ.
See how the babe grows and the mother shrivels
Five pulsing men and a little woman that bows
Nearer the earth each day. And the new corn bursts
Shouldering and splitting the rod and the husk blows empty
To be mashed in the mud.
It is not just the warmth we take from bodies
Leaving them bled cold on the mountain side
Not only calcium child draws from the bones.
Lapping the iron from the blood we take the spirit,
The strength the enemy had, the magic the hero.

The human being in his cave awaits
And waits to suck the image from the eye,
Absorb the sounds that come to the brain for music.
Cuckoo in nest sits with open mouth
To subvert the food
Not gut or blood alone but the strings of the mind
The pulse of the heart, the movement in the blood.
It is the vision that you make your world
That I must have or perish.
Your eye is not enough. Give me the mirror.

Man as real
(CITY; HUMAN)

Not stone, not air, but something in the air
More than the grit it carries.
Dried blood is only powder in the wind
Falling on fields to make plants grow; not that
Though we do come to that.

Little old woman who can speak no English
You therefore clutch my arm and ask with your face
(The thinker in stone stirs, the water ripples).

A lump of rock twizzling about in space
Has become a place where stacks of manure, produced
By cows, are harboured and outhouses kept dry
To hang up tools – clawhead, spirit-level;
Where men, waist-deep in the road, lift black handles
And telephone each other; and girls with pins
Knitting their lips, dress papier-mâché models.

                              the rock could fall
No other than it did; the mountain happened.
Our paraphernalia, – using wood for a ladder
Worms' hair for stockings, a ship for flight, a word
For a thing, made up – what is made, is made
By will against the grain, spire over gravity.

Not blood, not stone, bundled you stand beside me;
Not thought up; on this pavement, on this day
Merely there and offering
If not the flesh, then lustre from the flesh
If not the whirlwind some warmth travelling round
One to the other, current between two beings;
If not the source, then pool-lights bouncing back
Reflections, movement from the under-waters.

I have eaten, I am full this morning.
The earth is covered and the spring-splashed sky
Sucks scraps of paper up, and clatter of boxes,
And the thump and odour of streets, and flocks of people.
I have eaten and I breathe this air
And therefore you touch my shoulder and you ask

The way to Downshire road. The upland ether
Cannot supply us, so you lay your hand
Spent, haggy, kindly; your unshielded body,
That has more guts than all the beautiful tigers
Because it says
'Man, like the grass he is, battens on flesh
And as a piece of matter he lives, he dies.
Yet not off stone, life from the eyes this morning;
And not dead in the water all that you tell me.'

On the Embankment

On the one hand, the railings;
Railings, with shrubs behind,   sweet papers
Drifted against the bars with leaves and dog shit;
Variety of shrubs, labelled,   and paths
Statuary and fountain bowls,   hydrants,
People with clothes and gear, flower-patterns on dresses
Bags with letters in, park keepers, tea cups.

On the one hand the railings
                              and across the road
A long unbroken wall standing by itself.
The blank of fog fills all the space there is
Above the wall, and that is surrounded by nothing.

We are outside the railings, near colour and life
Trotting along the road, as if on a causeway.
Turn your head, there is nothing, no echo reflection,
All the commotion and plans that flesh this earth
Repulsed at the cut-off, it might be a thousand foot drop
At the end of land where only the elements
Let through the falling body.
You have to keep watching if you are to remember the land.
When you look away from the blindness above the river
The sudden busy scene looks like a picture:
Frame makes it unsubstantial, no connection.

And take another, this time summer, scene;
A polished chest of drawers, a lamp at night,
A jar of feathers, an inkwell in old wood,
Delicate indoor luxuries of the years
Fabricated, modelled, artefact.
And at waist level the polished black window beside:
A mantelpiece proceeding into trees,
The pretty lamp's tassels dangling in mid-air,
The feathers on a shed roof in a garden
That comes and goes in this mirror as you move.
It does not fade – the rest of the room just ceases
Just does not exist, one end of the chest not there
Like a statue with no back.   Empty unfurnished

The thick dark is a gulf.
No shed no trees no washing line no stars.
The dark has swallowed the lighted room and the things
And has made our frail fabric a playing of beams in a bubble
That a move of the head might extinguish.

Dark does not follow day, nor bleak winter summer
Time is two countries using the same space
One within the other, always there.
We walk a narrow path between the two
But cannot leave either, on our one hand blind

On the other the railings.

Index of titles and first lines

(Titles are in italics, first lines in roman type.)